THE WAY PEOPLE LIVE

Life Among the Aztecs

Titles in The Way People Live series include:

Cowboys in the Old West
Games of Ancient Rome
Life Aboard the Space Shuttle
Life Among the Aztecs
Life Among the Great Plains Indians
Life Among the Ibo Women of Nigeria
Life Among the Indian Fighters
Life Among the Pirates
Life Among the Puritans
Life Among the Samurai
Life Among the Vikings
Life During the American Revolution
Life During the Black Death
Life During the Crusades
Life During the Dust Bowl
Life During the French Revolution
Life During the Gold Rush
Life During the Great Depression
Life During the Middle Ages
Life During the Renaissance
Life During the Roaring Twenties
Life During the Russian Revolution
Life During the Spanish Inquisition
Life in a Japanese American
    Internment Camp
Life in a Medieval Castle
Life in a Medieval Monastery
Life in a Medieval Village
Life in America During the 1960s
Life in an Amish Community
Life in a Nazi Concentration Camp
Life in Ancient Athens
Life in Ancient China
Life in Ancient Egypt
Life in Ancient Greece

Life in Ancient Rome
Life in a Wild West Show
Life in Berlin
Life in Charles Dickens's England
Life in Communist Russia
Life in Genghis Khan's Mongolia
Life in Hong Kong
Life in Moscow
Life in the Amazon Rain Forest
Life in the American Colonies
Life in the Australian Outback
Life in the Elizabethan Theater
Life in the Hitler Youth
Life in the North During the Civil War
Life in the South During the Civil War
Life in the Warsaw Ghetto
Life in Tokyo
Life in War-Torn Bosnia
Life of a Medieval Knight
Life of a Nazi Soldier
Life of a Roman Gladiator
Life of a Roman Slave
Life of a Roman Soldier
Life of a Slave on a Southern Plantation
Life on Alcatraz
Life on a Medieval Pilgrimage
Life on an African Slave Ship
Life on an Everest Expedition
Life on Ellis Island
Life on the American Frontier
Life on the Oregon Trail
Life on the Pony Express
Life on the Underground Railroad
Life Under the Jim Crow Laws

THE WAY PEOPLE LIVE

Life Among the Aztecs

by Eleanor J. Hall

LUCENT
BOOKS ®

THOMSON

GALE

San Diego • Detroit • New York • San Francisco • Cleveland • New Haven, Conn. • Waterville, Maine • London • Munich

© 2004 by Lucent Books. Lucent Books is an imprint of The Gale Group, Inc., a division of Thomson Learning, Inc.

Lucent Books® and Thomson Learning™ are trademarks used herein under license.

For more information, contact
Lucent Books
27500 Drake Rd.
Farmington Hills, MI 48331-3535
Or you can visit our Internet site at http://www.gale.com

LIBRARY OF CONGRESS CATALOGING-IN-PUBLICATION DATA

Hall, Eleanor J.
    Life among the Aztec / by author, Eleanor J. Hall.
      p. cm. — (The way people live)
Includes bibliographical references.
    ISBN 1-59018-160-3
    1. Aztecs—History. 2. Aztecs—Social life and customs. I. Title. II. Series.
F1219.73H35 2004
972—dc22
                                        200400038

Printed in the United States of America

Contents

Discovering the Humanity in Us All

Books in The Way People Live series focus on groups of people in a wide variety of circumstances, settings, and time periods. Some books focus on different cultural groups, others, on people in a particular historical time period, while others cover people involved in a specific event. Each book emphasizes the daily routines, personal and historical struggles, and achievements of people from all walks of life.

To really understand any culture, it is necessary to strip the mind of the common notions we hold about groups of people. These stereotypes are the archenemies of learning. It does not even matter whether the stereotypes are positive or negative; they are confining and tight. Removing them is a challenge that is not easily met, as anyone who has ever tried it will admit. Ideas that do not fit into the templates we create are unwelcome visitors—ones we would prefer remain quietly in a corner or forgotten room.

The cowboy of the Old West is a good example of such confining roles. The cowboy was courageous, yet soft-spoken. His time (it is always a he, in our template) was spent alternatively saving a rancher's daughter from certain death on a runaway stagecoach, or shooting it out with rustlers. At times, of course, he was likely to get a little crazy in town after a trail drive, but for the most part, he was the epitome of inner strength. It is disconcerting to find out that the cowboy is human, even a bit childish. Can it really be true that cowboys would line up to help the cook on the trail drive grind coffee, just hoping he would give them a little stick of peppermint candy that came with the coffee shipment? The idea of tough cowboys vying with one another to help "Coosie" (as they called their cooks) for a bit of candy seems silly and out of place.

So is the vision of Eskimos playing video games and watching MTV, living in prefab housing in the Arctic. It just does not fit with what "Eskimo" means. We are far more comfortable with snow igloos and whale blubber, harpoons and kayaks.

Although the cultures dealt with in Lucent's The Way People Live series are often historically and socially well known, the emphasis is on the personal aspects of life. Groups of people, while unquestionably affected by their politics and their governmental structures, are more than those institutions. How do people in a particular time and place educate their children? What do they eat? And how do they build their houses? What kinds of work do they do? What kinds of games do they enjoy? The answers to these questions bring these cultures to life. People's lives are revealed in the particulars and only by knowing the particulars can we understand these cultures' will to survive and their moments of weakness and greatness.

This is not to say that understanding politics does not help to understand a culture. There is no question that the Warsaw ghetto, for example, was a culture that was brought about by the politics and social ideas of Adolf

Hitler and the Third Reich. But the Jews who were crowded together in the ghetto cannot be understood by the Reich's politics. Their life was a day-to-day battle for existence, and the creativity and methods they used to prolong their lives is a vital story of human perseverance that would be denied by focusing only on the institutions of Hitler's Germany. Knowing that children as young as five or six outwitted Nazi guards on a daily basis, that Jewish policemen helped the Germans control the ghetto, that children attended secret schools in the ghetto and even earned diplomas—these are the things that reveal the fabric of life, that can inspire, intrigue, and amaze.

Books in The Way People Live series allow both the casual reader and the student to see humans as victims, heroes, and onlookers. And although humans act in ways that can fill us with feelings of sorrow and revulsion, it is important to remember that "hero," "predator," and "victim" are dangerous terms. Heaping undue pity or praise on people reduces them to objects, and strips them of their humanity.

Seeing the Jews of Warsaw only as victims is to deny their humanity. Seeing them only as they appear in surviving photos, staring at the camera with infinite sadness, is limiting, both to them and to those who want to understand them. To an object of pity, the only appropriate response becomes "Those poor creatures!" and that reduces both the quality of their struggle and the depth of their despair. No one is served by such two-dimensional views of people and their cultures.

With this in mind, The Way People Live series strives to flesh out the traditional, two-dimensional views of people in various cultures and historical circumstances. Using a wide variety of primary quotations—the words not only of the politicians and government leaders, but of the real people whose lives are being examined—each book in the series attempts to show an honest and complete picture of a culture removed from our own by time or space.

By examining cultures in this way, the reader will notice not only the glaring differences from his or her own culture, but also will be struck by the similarities. For indeed, people share common needs—warmth, good company, stability, and affirmation from others. Ultimately, seeing how people really live, or have lived, can only enrich our understanding of ourselves.

Beginnings

The Aztecs were the last of many complex civilizations that rose and fell in Mesoamerica before Europeans arrived there in the fifteenth century. The early recorded history of the Aztecs is a mixture of real events and mythological accounts, making it difficult to pinpoint where they originated. What is known for certain, however, is that groups of seminomadic peoples began migrating into the Valley of Mexico from the highlands to the north sometime during the twelfth century. Collectively known as Chichimecs, these bands shared similar cultural backgrounds and considered their homeland to be a place called Aztlan. Whether Aztlan was a real or a mythical place is not known.

Migration and Settlement

One group of Chichimecs, the Mexicas, arrived in the Valley of Mexico after all the prime land in the valley had been taken. For a while, they were forced to wander from one place to another seeking a homeland. According to Aztec legends, their patron god, Huitzilopochtli, told them to settle at a place where they saw an eagle with a snake in its mouth perched on a cactus. Shortly thereafter, the promised eagle appeared on an island in Lake Texcoco, a swampy area that no one else wanted. There the Mexicas settled and built Tenochtitlán, their capital city.

To survive, the newcomers paid tribute and served as mercenaries for more powerful tribes already there. By the early fourteenth century, however, the determined Mexicas had built a power base of their own and subdued all their regional rivals. Through political strategy, intermarriage, and warfare, the Mexicas gradually expanded their territory into an extensive empire. The name *Aztec* was applied to this empire much later by scholars to include all Chichimec groups claiming Aztlan as their place of origin.

By warfare, political strategy, and trading, the Aztecs dominated central Mexico for at least a century before the Spanish conquistadores arrived. Historian Richard F. Townsend writes, "By November 1519 [when Cortés arrived] . . . the Aztecs had successfully built what may have been the largest empire in Mesoamerican history. A century had seen a continuous advance of their power, as the warlords engaged in campaigns of conquest and in forming dominant relations with neighboring peoples."[1]

Sources of Information

Information about the Aztec Empire and its people comes from many different sources. One important source is the Aztecs themselves. Over time, the Aztecs developed a writing system that used pictures and ideograms to commemorate important events, preserve official documents, and tell stories. The pictures were painted in bright colors on long strips of paper made from natural fibers, cloth, or animal skins. The strips were then folded accordion-style to form books. Unfortunately, none of these books survived the conquest of the empire by Spain in 1521.

However, several books were re-created in the traditional style by Aztec scribes after the conquest, and a few of these still exist. In addition, a number of Aztec scholars wrote

The Aztecs developed a sophisticated writing system using pictures and ideograms, examples of which are seen on this page from a syllabary compiled by Spanish scribes.

their own history in Nahuatl, the Aztec language that was written down for the first time after the conquest.

Other major sources of information about the Aztecs come from Spanish authors. These include five letters to the king of Spain from Spanish conquistador Hernán Cortés; a memoir of the conquest by Bernal Díaz del Castillo, one of Cortés's soldiers; and a book about Aztec culture by an author who signed himself only as "a companion of Cortés." Spanish priests who came to Mexico as missionaries also wrote books with detailed descriptions of Aztec life and culture. Although all of these sources reflect the cultural biases of their writers, together they provide valuable information about Aztec life.

Useful information also comes from official records and documents kept by Spanish colonial administrators. These documents include birth, death, and baptismal certificates and land distribution records. Equally valuable for scholars are reports originally compiled to help new Spanish administrators understand Aztec culture.

Still another source of information is archaeology. Much may be learned about the Aztecs from the ruins of their settlements and from the arts and crafts they left behind. Traditionally, archaeological excavations in Mexico have concentrated on spectacular urban sites and the lives of elite members of Aztec society. One such focal point is Mexico City, which was built over the ruins of the Aztec

The Memoirs of Bernal Díaz del Castillo

Bernal Díaz del Castillo was a Spanish soldier who served under Hernán Cortés throughout a two-year struggle to overthrow the Aztec Empire. Díaz del Castillo began writing the story of the conquest when he was past seventy years of age. His eyewitness account of the Aztec Empire at its zenith is considered a classic today. In this excerpt from *The Conquest of New Spain*, Díaz del Castillo describes the entry of Cortés and his army into the capital city of the Aztec Empire and the meeting of Cortés with Montezuma, the Aztec emperor.

"When we came near to Mexico [Tenochtitlan, the Aztec capital city] . . . the great Montezuma descended from his litter [carriage balanced on men's shoulders], and these other *Caciques* supported him beneath a marvelously rich canopy of green feathers decorated with gold work, silver, and pearls, which hung from a sort of border. It was a marvelous sight. The great Montezuma was

magnificently clad, in their fashion, and wore sandals . . . the soles of which are gold and the uppers parts ornamented with precious stones. When Cortés saw, heard, and was told that the great Montezuma was approaching, he dismounted his horse, and when he came near to Montezuma, each bowed deeply to the other. Montezuma welcomed our captain, and Cortés, speaking through Dona Maria [an Indian interpreter accompanying Cortés], answered by wishing him very good health. . . . Then Cortés brought out a necklace which he had been holding. . . . This he hung round the great Montezuma's neck, and as he did so attempted to embrace him. But the great princes who stood round Montezuma grasped Cortés' arm to prevent him, for they considered this an indignity."

Complimentary speeches were then exchanged between the two leaders, and Montezuma ordered his men to escort the Spaniards to their quarters in the city.

capital city after the Spanish conquest in 1521. Many significant archaeological discoveries have been made in Mexico City, mostly relating to the power and glory of the Aztec Empire.

Today, however, many archaeologists are turning to rural Aztec sites outside of Mexico City to learn more about the common people on whose shoulders the success of the empire rested. One such archaeologist is Michael E. Smith, who explains the importance of studying the common people:

> Pyramids and palaces were certainly important parts of ancient cultures, but so were peasant houses, foods and crops, merchants and markets, and other aspects of everyday life that the monumental archaeology approach omits. The social archaeology approach depends upon the principle that everyday actions of ordinary people are important parts of any culture. These things can be reconstructed for the Aztecs or any ancient civilization if the appropriate methods and theories are used to guide archaeological fieldwork and analysis.[2]

This new focus is already yielding greater appreciation of the skills and ingenuity of the Aztec as they went about their daily lives. "Now outside of Mexico City, more archaeologists than ever are digging Aztec sites," writes art historian Elizabeth Hill Boone. "More scholars from a wide range of disciplines—including anthropology, history, art history, religious studies, archaeoastronomy, and ethnobotany—are working comparatively to integrate the archaeological and documentary records. . . . For all that has been written about the Aztecs by the conquerors, chroniclers, and native historians, the archaeological record still holds some surprises."[3]

The Aztec People: Family and Society

Before Europeans arrived in the New World, all the people in Mexico were descended from the first inhabitants of the New World who migrated from Asia. The Aztecs shared certain physical characteristics with their Asian ancestors. Their skin tones ranged in color from tan to brown. Their faces were broad with prominent noses and dark eyes, and their hair was black and straight. The Aztecs were short in stature, the men averaging about five feet, seven inches, and the women about four feet, ten inches. Both men and women had strong physiques and were capable of great physical endurance and hard work.

Aztec Grooming and Fashion

Women wore their hair long, but on important occasions they braided it with colorful ribbons and wound it around their heads. Pictures of women in Aztec books show the ends of their braids sticking up like little horns on the tops of their heads. Men's hairstyles were very important because they signified status and rank. "Men usually wore [their hair] cut in a fringe over the forehead," writes anthropologist Warwick Bray, "and allowed it to grow to the level of the nape of the neck at the back, but the priests had their own distinctive hair style and the warriors wore pigtails and various kinds of scalp locks."[4] Men had sparse facial hair and rarely wore beards.

Personal hygiene was very important to the Aztecs. In his book about the everyday lives of the Aztecs, historian David Carrasco discusses some of the methods the people used to keep themselves clean and physically attractive. He writes:

> Aztec people enjoyed bathing and personal cleanliness, and they used the fruit of a soap tree and the roots of certain plants for soap. They took cold baths but were especially committed to steam baths. Many homes had steam bathhouses which have been excavated in the Basin of Mexico. These steambaths were used for ritual purification, during sicknesses, and to help pregnant women, but also as a part of daily hygiene.[5]

Women wore perfumes made from plants and chewed gum to sweeten the breath. Fashionable Aztec women used various cosmetics to enhance their appearance. These included face powder made from ground yellow ochre and a red dye called cochineal to stain the teeth. Cochineal are red scale insects that live on the pads of certain cactus plants. The Aztecs harvested the insects, then dried and crushed them to make this important cosmetic dye, which was also used to dye fabrics. The Aztecs even made mirrors of polished obsidian glass to aid them in their grooming.

Clothing

As in most societies, the quality and richness of the clothing worn by the Aztecs differed greatly according to social class. However, the basic style of dress was very much the same for all classes. Men wore a loincloth, which passed between their legs and around their waists, where it was tied with decorative knots front and back. Sometimes they wore nothing at all on their upper bodies, but for greater warmth or protection they wore a cloak or mantle tied in a knot at one shoulder. For women, the traditional garb was a wrap-around skirt held up by a colorful sash and topped with a simple blouse. Blouses were made from two pieces of cloth sewn together with holes left open for head and arms.

Class distinctions in clothing were so important to the Aztecs that laws were issued reserving certain kinds of clothing and personal adornments for the privileged classes. For example, commoners were forbidden to wear cotton clothing and sandals, even if they could afford them. The clothing of commoners was made from fibers of the maguey cactus plant and decorated as elaborately as the law and their personal finances allowed. Members of the nobility wore garments woven in intricate patterns, richly embroidered, and trimmed with feathers,

This highly stylized illustration of Aztec warriors battling before a group of onlookers clearly shows the loincloth worn by the men of all classes of Aztec society.

This print shows a cross-section of an Aztec steam bath, or sauna, one of the Aztecs' favorite diversions.

gemstones, gold, and silver. Some of their garments were made entirely of featherwork in vivid colors and beautiful designs.

Nobles wore necklaces and bracelets made of gold, silver, and gemstones on their arms and ankles. Noble men pierced their ears, gradually making the holes larger to insert ornaments of jade, obsidian, and precious metals. They also inserted lip plugs through holes pierced under their bottom lips, and nose plugs in holes on the sides of their noses. Sometimes a thin metal rod was stuck through the septum, the fleshy section of the nose between the nostrils. Elaborately trimmed headdresses also served as status symbols for the nobility, and laws decreed

who was eligible to wear certain kinds.

Common people enjoyed wearing jewelry also, but they had to make do with less costly materials, such as polished stones, beads, bones, and shells. Differences in clothing and ornamentation between rich and poor classes were just a small part of the differences in the Aztec social classes. Class distinctions played a significant role in every aspect of Aztec life.

Noble Social Classes

At the top of the Aztec social structure was a supreme ruler called *tlatloani* in the language of the Aztecs. Although the position of *tlatloani* was hereditary through the male line, it did not pass rigidly from father to son. Rather, it was conferred on a relative of the former *tlatloani* by a council of nobles who also held inherited positions. The successor chosen by the council might well be a son, but it also could be a brother, uncle, nephew, or grandson, depending upon the personal qualifications of the successor. Other important people in the upper ranks of society were governmental officials and advisers to the *tlatloani* as well as high-ranking priests in the Aztec religious system. This arrangement was repeated with

Members of the highest social classes (pictured is Emperor Montezuma II) wore jewelry made of gold, silver, and gemstones, and had pierced ears and lips.

less power and prestige in city-states that made up the Aztec Empire. A king or chieftain and his own group of nobles ruled each city-state. Historic documents make it clear that upper-class men filled all the highest government positions in the city-states. At local levels of government, women occasionally served as chieftains or *caciques*. Altogether, the upper classes consisted of only 5 percent of the population, but their lack of numbers did not reduce their power over the common people.

Common Social Classes

The majority of the population consisted of the common people, but they, too, were stratified into subclasses based mainly on occupation. People in all subclasses were affiliated with a *calpulli*, a sort of clan under the authority of a noble. The *calpulli* was where all important matters in the lives of the common people took place. *Calpulli* officials assigned farming lands, conscripted men for military service and public works, built and maintained schools and temples, collected tribute for the emperor, and generally looked after the welfare of its members.

Near the bottom of the social system were *mayeques*, poor peasants who, for various reasons, had no *calpulli* affiliation. *Mayeques* usually worked as serfs on the estates of the nobility. All subclasses of commoners, no matter how lowly, were free citizens. However, at the very bottom of the social structure were slaves, most of whom served Aztec nobles and lords in their palaces or worked on their estates. Archaeologist Michael E. Smith describes a variety of ways in which an Aztec might become a slave:

People became slaves through debt or punishment, but not through birth; slavery

Rising in the Social System

The Aztec social class system was quite rigid and there were only a few ways in which a commoner could experience upward mobility. One of these was through valorous actions on the battlefield. In the following excerpt from *Aztecs of Mexico: Origin, Rise and Fall of the Aztec Nation*, author George C. Vaillant describes what a warrior had to do to rise in the social class system.

"Since the capture of victims for sacrifice was the chief glory of war, an able soldier who could subdue his enemies and drag them to the rear received much honor. According to the number of captives taken, a warrior had the right to wear an increasingly elaborate costume. Consistently successful warriors could enter an order . . . which performed special dances and rituals. Sometimes a warrior of unusual prowess received additional grants of land or more often obtained an increased portion of the clan's share of tribute. Having reached an established position by this means, he had a more important voice in clan councils and might attain a seat in the council itself. A specific honorific, *tecuhtli* (grandfather), which corresponds to chief among the North American Indians, distinguished these men. The title signified high social, but not official, rank, and from these men who had distinguished themselves by probity, bravery and religious observance, high elective and appointive posts were filled."

was not hereditary. Slaves could marry, have children (who were free), and even own property. Anyone could own a slave, but most slave owners were nobles. . . . People sold themselves into slavery when they could not support themselves. . . . Some people incurred such large debts through gambling . . . that selling themselves was the only way out. Failure to pay tribute was another way to become a slave, with the purchase price going to cover the tribute debt. . . . The change in status from free citizen to slave was an official act that had to be witnessed formally by four officials. Slaves either then began work for their master or were sold in the market.[6]

Social Mobility

As rigid as the system was, there were still a few ways to achieve upward mobility. One of these was to become a distinguished warrior by capturing live prisoners in battle for sacrificial ceremonies. The more captives a warrior brought back, the greater were the honors given to him. Another way to move up socially was through the priesthood. Anyone could become a priest, women as well as men, but the training was difficult and the priestly life was hard.

Commoners who enjoyed more freedom and privileges than any of the others were the *pochteca*, long-distance merchants. The status of this group rose as the empire grew larger and more dependent on products from outlying regions. These traveling merchants supplied the nobility with highly prized goods, such as cocoa, jade, gold, and precious feathers. The merchants themselves were allowed to become rich as long as they did not show off their wealth. For that reason, they generally lived apart in special enclaves so as not to attract attention.

The Aztec Family

The fact that only 5 percent of the Aztec population was able to maintain tight control over the other 95 percent may be explained in part by the nature of the Aztec family. "An Aztec was never alone," writes art historian Elizabeth Hill Boone. "She or he always belonged to a household, a ward, and a community kingdom (town or city), and in these the individual found comfort and structure."[7]

Aztec children were trained to be obedient and to accept the position in life to which they were born. As children grew up, Aztec parents and other relatives continuously lectured them about the duties and responsibilities expected of them at various stages of their lives. They were taught to be honest and loyal, to revere the patron gods of their clans, and to behave properly in public.

Lectures such as these became standard and were passed down by word of mouth. Many pictures in Aztec books show adults with speech glyphs coming out of their mouths as they teach their children. A speech glyph is a mark that looks something like a tongue, curled under at the end, and signifying that a person is speaking. One such speech, advice from a father to his son, was recorded by Alonzo de Zorita, a governor of New Spain in the sixteenth century, as follows:

> Revere and greet your elders; console the poor and the afflicted with good works and words. . . . Follow not the madmen, who honour neither father or mother; for they are like animals, for they neither hear or take advice. . . . Do not

Commoners and slaves occupy the bottom rung of this illustration of the social structure of the Aztecs, while warriors and noblemen find themselves at the top.

mock the old, the sick, the maimed, or one who has sinned. Do not insult or abhor them, but abase yourself before God and fear lest the same befall you. . . . Do not set a bad example, or speak indiscreetly, or interrupt the speech of another, if someone does not speak well or coherently, see that you do not the same; if it is not your business to speak, be silent. If you are asked something, reply soberly and without affectation or flattery or prejudice to others, and your speech will be well regarded. . . . Wherever you go, walk with a peaceful air and do not make wry faces or improper gestures.[8]

Growing Up Aztec

Important family rituals beginning with the birth of a baby emphasized traditional gender and class roles. For example, a few days after a child was born, a naming ritual was held. If the newborn was a boy, a little arrow was tucked into his hand, and a symbol of his father's occupation was displayed beside him. After the ceremony, the boy's umbilical cord was buried at a place connected with a military event. If the baby was a girl, symbolic implements associated with weaving and housekeeping were displayed during the naming ritual. Her umbilical cord was buried under a metate, a slab of stone on which Aztec women ground corn.

By the age of four, boys were working alongside their fathers and girls were learning to spin cotton thread, help with cooking, and do other household chores. The *Codex Mendoza*, a handcrafted picture book created by Aztec scribes in the sixteenth century, illustrates the tasks boys and girls learned as they grew up. Pictures show a mother introducing the art of spinning thread to her daughter at the age of four. By the age of six, the little girl is doing it herself while her mother watches. Other illustrations in the *Codex Mendoza* show little boys carrying water in bowls at four years of age. At five they are carrying firewood and other heavy loads on their backs. By the age of seven, the boys in the illustrations are learning to fish with nets while their fathers look on. In all the illustrations, speech glyphs come out of the parents' mouths as they give instructions.

In addition to the rigorous training Aztec children received at home, free schools (separated by class and gender) were provided by local government units. Boys and girls attended school during their adolescent years until they married. Since Aztec women generally married at younger ages than men, women accordingly received less formal education than men.

Discipline

Although children were greatly prized, Aztec parents placed great emphasis on proper behavior. The *Codex Mendoza* shows how children who behave badly are punished. For instance, parents threaten their eight-year-old children by showing them pointed spines from the maguey cactus plant and telling them that the spines will be stuck in their flesh if they persist in bad behavior. The next set of pictures shows this actually happening. At the age of nine, a boy is tied hand and foot while his father pierces his ears and back with cactus spines. A girl's punishment at the same age shows the mother sticking her daughter's hand with a cactus spine.

Parents are shown beating both boys and girls with a stick for being deceitful, lazy, or unmanageable. At eleven a disobedient boy is held over a fire made from chili peppers and forced to inhale the fumes. A girl of the same age is held close to a fire and threatened with the same punishment if she does not behave. A boy of twelve is punished by being stripped naked, tied hand and foot, and left to spend the night on the cold ground, while a girl of twelve is forced to get up in the middle of the night to sweep the house or grind corn. From the age of twelve onward, illustrations show adolescents being forced to do extra work as punishment.

Marriage and Adult Life

With only a few exceptions, Aztec men and women were expected to marry. Young women were considered marriageable at the age of fifteen years, or even younger, while men were allowed to wait until their late teens or early twenties. When it was time for a son to marry, his parents and relatives selected a prospective bride from a suitable family. (Sometimes the husband-to-be already had a young lady in mind.) The boy's parents then obtained the services of a

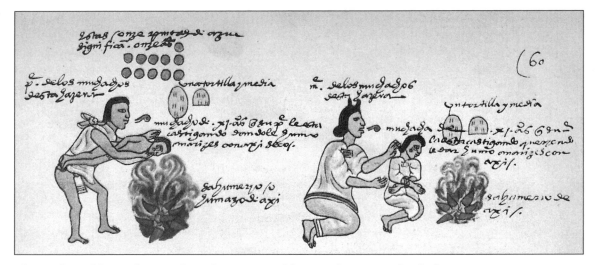

This replica of the Codex Mendosa shows some of the punishments with which Aztec children were threatened to ensure their good behavior.

matchmaker who contacted the family of the prospective bride.

In marriage negotiations, long-standing customs were followed. For example, when first approached by the matchmaker, the bride's family would insist that their daughter was too young, too immature, and really not worthy of so distinguished a person as the prospective husband. If the bride's family really desired the marriage, however, traditional negotiations continued and the marriage contract was made on the fourth day. The next step was to choose a date for the wedding. For this task, a soothsayer had to be consulted, because certain days in the Aztec calendar were felt to be unlucky for such an important event.

Once the date was set, preparations began for the festive occasion. Invitations were sent out and special foods and beverages were prepared for the guests. The ceremony began at the bride's home, where she was bathed and dressed in her finest clothes and made ready for the journey to the groom's home. As they dressed the bride, her kinswomen took

the opportunity to counsel her at length about her new life and domestic responsibilities. She was then carried to the groom's home on the back of one of her kinswomen in a torch-light parade.

At the groom's home, the couple was seated on a mat beside a small hearth in which a fire was lighted and incense burned. After speeches and gift giving by the parents, the matchmaker tied the bride's skirt to the groom's cloak, signifying that they were now united in marriage. Following the marriage ceremony, the fun and feasting went on for four days. During this time the bride and groom were sequestered in a room to get to know each other, but were forbidden to have sexual relations until after the four-day ceremony was over.

Of course, not all marriages turned out well. Aztec law recognized this fact by allowing divorce for certain causes. A man could divorce his wife if she were sterile, if she neglected her marriage and household duties, or if she was ill-tempered. A wife could obtain a divorce from a husband if he did not support her and their children or if he mistreated her physically. Divorced men and women were free to remarry.

Rulers often had multiple wives as well as concubines. One of Cortés's soldiers, Bernal Díaz del Castillo, reports that Emperor Montezuma "had many women as his mistresses, the daughters of chieftains, but two legitimate wives who were [rulers] in their own right."[9] Polygamy also occurred in the lower classes, possibly because the death of so many men in battle caused an unequal ratio of women to men.

Sexuality

In matters of sexuality, women were expected to remain faithful to their husbands while men were allowed more sexual freedom as long as they did not consort with married women. For people found guilty of adultery, the punishment for both parties was death. The man's head was crushed with a stone, and the woman was strangled, regardless of social class.

As a rule, the Aztecs were conservative in their personal lives, but early accounts from

This illustration details the steps involved in the Aztec marriage ceremony. After being carried to the groom's home on a kinswoman's back (w), the bride has her shirt tied to the groom's cloak (center).

both Aztec and Spanish sources make it clear that departures from ideal sexual behavior (as the Aztecs defined it) occurred in Aztec society. For example, prostitution was allowed and even organized. According to anthropologist Inga Clendinnen, "The pleasure girls from the Houses of Joy were . . . symbols of sexuality and eroticism, dancing with the young warriors, hair unbound and faces bare to men's glances. . . . We know almost nothing of their conditions of life, save that they were under the close jurisdiction of 'matrons' responsible for their public decorum and for negotiating their private assignations."[10]

Amusements

Although Aztec life in general was structured and orderly, some leisure activities afforded a break in the daily routine. One of these was a ball game called *tlachtli*. It was mainly a spectator sport played on special ball courts by professional teams, by groups of nobles, or sometimes by just two opponents. According to historian Richard F. Townsend, the ball game had many purposes: "The popular ball-game—dating back to the beginnings of civilization in Mesoamerica—was played for sport and gambling, for resolving disputes, and as a form of divination."[11] In the latter case, ball games were often played to foretell the outcome of important matters of state. Ball courts were built close to the temples and their architectural design represented the universe.

The object of the ball game was to pass a hard rubber ball through a small ring protruding from a slanted wall on each side of a ball court. The players could move the ball only with their hips, knees, and elbows, and since few players ever actually put the ball through the hoop, points were scored for other maneuvers as well. If anyone actually did put the ball through the hoop, his team immediately won the game and the man who scored the goal was allowed to confiscate the cloaks and other possessions of all those watching the game—that is, if he could catch them. "This was not an easy custom to enforce," comments Bray, "and everybody scrambled for the exit while the player and his friends tried to grab as many people as they could."[12]

A popular game in which all classes of people participated was *patolli*. The rules were complicated. Players threw beans on a mat on which a diagram was drawn, and winners and losers were determined by where the beans landed on the diagram. *Patolli* also had a winner-take-all feature. Anyone whose bean stood on end when it landed could confiscate the possessions of the other players. As in the ball game, heavy wagering usually accompanied the game of *patolli* when played by adults. Children had their own form of this popular game.

Old Age

The life expectancy for Aztec males was probably only about forty years of age. As in all societies, some Aztec individuals lived well beyond that age. Therefore, to become old in Aztec society was a feat that carried certain privileges with it. One of the most unusual of these was the freedom to get drunk. Drinking itself was not condemned in Aztec society as long as one did not overdo it. Drunkenness, however, was despised by the Aztecs because it made the drinker lose the self-discipline so highly regarded in Aztec culture. Elderly people, however, were exempt from this strict rule. Usually they drank a relatively mild intoxicant made from fermented cactus sap.

The Aztec Fashion Police

Diego Duran was a Spanish priest of the Dominican order who lived and worked among the Aztec in the late sixteenth century. He was a learned man and anxious that the history and culture of the Aztecs should not be lost. He therefore undertook to save as much as possible by interviewing Aztec nobles and commoners, examining Aztec records, and reading accounts of the conquest. He then compiled three books about the Aztecs that present a remarkably objective account of Aztec life and culture. In the following excerpt from *The History of the Indies of New Spain* (translated and edited by Fernando Horcasitas and Doris Heyden), Duran tells how wearing the wrong thing in Aztec society could be a matter of life and death.

"Chapter XXVI Which Treats of the Laws, Ordinances and Statutes Decreed by King Moteczuma I in the City of Mexico

Because Mexico was now at peace, living in order and tranquility, King Moteczuma gathered together all the chieftains of Mexico and the allied states and decreed the following laws for the future.

- Only the king may wear a golden diadem [headdress] in the city, though in war all the great lords and brave captains may wear such. It is considered that those who go to war represent the royal person.

- Only the king and the Prime Minister Tlacaelel may wear sandals within the palace. No great chieftain may enter the palace shod, under pain of death. The great noblemen are the only ones to be allowed to wear sandals in the city and no one else, with the exception of men who have performed some great deed in war. But these sandals must be cheap and common; the gilded, painted ones are to be worn only by noblemen.

- Only the king is to wear the fine mantles [cloaks] of cotton embroidered with designs and threads of different colors and featherwork.

- The common soldier may wear only the simplest type of mantle and is prohibited from using any special designs or fine embroidery that might set him off from the rest.

- The common people will not be allowed to wear cotton clothing, under pain of death, but only garments of maguey [cactus plant] fiber. The mantle must not be worn below the knee and if anyone allows it to reach the ankle, he will be killed, unless he has wounds of war on his legs. [Duran adds, 'And so it was that when one encountered a person who wore his mantle longer than the law permitted, one immediately looked at his legs. If he had wounds acquired in war he would be left in peace, and if he did not, he would be killed.']

- Only the great lords are to wear lip-plugs, ear-plugs and nose-plugs of gold and precious stones, except strong men, brave captains and soldiers, but their ornaments must be of bone, wood or other inferior materials.

- Only the king and the sovereigns of the provinces and other great lords are to wear gold arm-bands, anklets, and golden rattles on their feet at the dances. They may wear garlands and headbands with feathers in them in the style they desire, and no one else."

Called pulque or *octli*, this drink had an alcohol content similar to wine or beer.

Death

Aztec society was characterized by constant wars and frequent religious sacrifices. Death was highly visible. Capital punishment was carried out in public, and crowds of worshipers witnessed human sacrifices that accompanied religious festivals. In warfare, the population of entire towns was often wiped out, women and children included. Of course, people also died of accidents, disease, and old age.

From birth to death, the Aztec people were closely bound to their society. The class system, the family, and the training of children played important roles in helping the nobility maintain control over thousands of commoners. In addition, stability and order were maintained by the political organization of the empire.

2 Government and Law

From its beginning, the Aztec Empire was a work in progress. Power struggles among rivals and wars to acquire new territory were ongoing occurrences. About a century before the Spanish conquest, three major groups vied for supremacy—the Mexicas, Tenochas, and Acolhuas. Their territories adjoined each other, with the Mexicas situated between the other two. To balance the power and reduce the frequency of wars, these three groups formed the Triple Alliance in the early fifteenth century. However, the Mexicas dominated the alliance, eventually becoming undisputed lords of the Valley of Mexico and many other territories beyond the confines of the valley.

The Capital City at Tenochtitlán

The most visible symbol of Aztec supremacy was Tenochtitlán, the capital city built on an island in Lake Texcoco. In the early years after its founding, Tenochtitlán was much like other towns in the region. As the Mexicas grew more powerful, however, they completely rebuilt the city to reflect their beliefs and demonstrate their power. Archaeologist Michael E. Smith comments:

> First they used a grid layout . . . to establish a common alignment for all buildings. Second, they effected a radical change in the layout of the downtown area by walling off a sacred precinct from the rest

of the city. Third, they deliberately copied architectural and sculptural styles from Teotihuacan and Tula [ancient cities nearby] in their rebuilt downtown area. . . . Unlike the haphazard layouts of most towns and cities, the entire urban area of Tenochtitlan was carefully planned and rebuilt according to fundamental political, religious, and practical principles.[13]

At its peak, the population of Tenochtitlán was around two hundred thousand people or perhaps more. A great temple stood in the center of the city, a high, flat-topped pyramid of stone on which stood two shrines—one to Huitzilopochtli, patron god of the Aztecs, and the other to Tlaloc, god of rain and fertility. It was here that the Aztecs publicly sacrificed thousands of captives to their patron gods to discourage rebellion and further demonstrate their superiority.

Governmental Structure

Around the main temple were civic buildings and luxurious palaces where the emperor and other high-status members of the nobility resided. The highest official in the government was the emperor. In the Nahuatl language, he was a *tlatloani*, meaning "first speaker." The *tlatloani* occupied the office of external affairs, whose major function was to expand and consolidate the empire. Authority was also vested in a chief of internal affairs,

Lake Texcoco stretches beyond Tenochtitlán, the capital of the Aztec empire and the site of modern-day Mexico City.

similar to a prime minister. The person in this position also wielded a lot of power. For instance, during the outstanding reign of Montezuma I, the chief of internal affairs was Montezuma's half brother, Tlacaelel. The two brothers, along with Nezahualcoyotl, king of the neighboring city-state of Texcoco, played major roles in forming the Triple Alliance and expanding the Aztec Empire.

In addition to the two top positions, the Aztec governmental structure included a council of nobles, high priests who oversaw important religious functions, and a staff of distinguished warriors who directed the army. These positions provided checks and balances on the emperor's authority by means of advice and persuasion or even outright removal of an undesired monarch if necessary. As the em-

pire grew larger and more powerful, however, the authority of the *tlatloani* grew with it. Describing this change, historian Richard F. Townsend writes, "By the time of Cortes' arrival, the external affairs chief had all but assumed the character of a tyrant, wielding both inside and outside powers. This is why the Spanish regarded [Montezuma II] as an absolute king."[14]

Montezuma II

Montezuma II (the great-grandson of Montezuma I) certainly looked and acted the part of an absolute king according to a description of him given by Bernal Díaz del Castillo, one of Cortés's soldiers. Díaz del Castillo writes:

The great Montezuma was about forty years old, of good height, well proportioned, spare and slight, and not very dark, though of the usual Indian complexion. He did not wear his hair long but just over his ears, and he had a short black beard, well shaped and thin. His face was rather long and cheerful, he had fine eyes, and in his appearance and manner could express geniality or, when necessary, a serious composure.[15]

Díaz del Castillo tells how important Aztec chieftains who came to see the emperor had to take off their sandals and put on cheap cloaks before they entered his chambers. Once in his presence, they kept their eyes cast downward, bowed three times, and stated their business. Montezuma answered them very briefly and they backed from the room, still keeping their eyes on the floor.

Díaz del Castillo also devotes many pages of his memoirs to descriptions of Montezuma's palaces, his gardens, and the entertainers that amused him. "There were dancers and stilt-walkers, and some who seemed to fly as they leapt through the air," Díaz del Castillo reports, "and men rather like clowns to make him laugh. There was a whole quarter full of these people who had no other occupation."[16]

Montezuma's Zoo

Upon entering Tenochtitlán for the first time, Cortés and his men were utterly amazed by the sights in the city and even more so by the lifestyle of the emperor, Montezuma II. In one of his letters to the king of Spain, Captain Cortés describes the collections of live animals and birds that were kept in various palaces for the emperor's amusement. This excerpt is taken from *Five Letters 1519–1526* by Hernán Cortés and translated from the Spanish by J. Bayard Morris.

"He possessed many houses of recreation both within and without the city, each with its own special pastime, built in the most ingenious manner as was fitting for such a mighty prince: of which I will say no more than that there is not their like in all Spain. Another palace of his (not quite so fine as the one we were lodged in) had a magnificent garden with balconies overhanging it, the pillars and flagstones of which were all jasper beautifully worked. In this palace there was room to lodge two powerful princes with all their ret-inue. There were also ten pools of water in which were kept every kind of waterfowl known in these parts, fresh water being provided for the river birds, salt for those of the sea, and the water itself being frequently changed to keep it pure. . . . Each pool was overhung by balconies cunningly arranged, from which Montezuma would delight to watch the birds. . . . He also had another beautiful house in which there was a large courtyard, paved very prettily with flagstones in the manner of a chessboard. In this palace were cages some nine feet high and six yards round: each of these was half covered with tiles and the other half by a wooden trellis skillfully made. They contained birds of prey, and there was an example of every one that is known in Spain, from kestrel to eagle, and many others which were new to us. . . . Other large rooms on the ground floor were full of cages made of stout wood very firmly put together and containing large numbers of lions, tigers, wolves, foxes and wild cats of various kinds."

Aztec conqueror Hernán Cortés wrote lengthy letters to the king of Spain in which he described the luxurious lifestyle of Emperor Montezuma. Cortés was amazed that a man he considered a barbarian had such a magnificent lifestyle. He reported that Montezuma changed his splendid garments four times a day, bathed frequently, and never ate from the same dishes twice. Both Cortés and Díaz del Castillo also noted Montezuma's awesome personal power. For instance, simply looking into his face was punishable by death, for the great emperor was thought to be a direct representative of the gods.

City-States

Outside of Tenochtitlán, about fifty city-states with similar cultures and language made up the core of the Aztec empire. Each city-state had its own ruler, who was chosen by a council of nobles. Rulers of city-states were allowed to govern their territories as long as they remained loyal to the emperor, enforced the empire's laws, and sent regular tribute to Tenochtitlán.

Controlling an empire in this fashion was risky, especially on the fringes of the empire. To the Aztecs, however, the cost of colonizing conquered areas and setting up new governments in them far outweighed the benefits. Brutally punishing rebellious or disobedient city-states as a deterrent to others was a preferred tactic. In his book about Aztec warfare, anthropologist Ross Hassig provides an example:

> The people of Oztoman refused to pay tribute to the Aztecs, so the army attacked, broke through the fortifications, burned the temple, and killed the people, sparing only the children. Then they sent

emissaries to Alahuiztlan asking for tribute, which the town refused to give, and the Aztec attacked and razed that city as well. All the adults were killed in Alahuiztlan and Oztoman, and more than forty thousand children were taken and distributed throughout the rest of the empire. . . . The campaign itself encouraged submission by demonstrating that the fate of the conquered cities was partially in the hands of the vanquished: those who cooperated received more favorable treatment than those who did not.[17]

Many of the city-states maintained impressive capital cities within their boundaries. The downtown areas of these cities were similar to that of Tenochtitlán, but on a much more modest scale. A temple, civic buildings, and nobles' residences occupied the center, but beyond that, city life and rural life were not much different. Smith writes, "Most Aztec cities were quite 'rural' in appearance, owing to their unplanned residential districts, farming within the urban site, the presence of large houselots, and an overall low population density. Outside of the downtown area, cities did not look much different from towns and villages."[18]

Tribute

Although certain items (such as cacao beans and bolts of cloth) were sometimes used as a medium of exchange, the Aztecs had no formal currency system. Tribute, therefore, was paid in the form of goods and services. The goods owed to the emperor were determined by the natural resources of each area and included cloaks (called mantles), tunics, skirts, war dresses, shields, deer skins, gold, amber, jade, turquoise, ornamental feathers, copper

Spanish visitors to the court of Montezuma II (pictured) were astonished by the incredibly luxurious lifestyle the Aztec emperor led.

ax heads, copal (a resin from various tropical trees), cactus honey, wooden planks for construction, wood for fuel, pottery, paper, and bins of grain and salt. These goods were collected and taken on the backs of porters to Tenochtitlán at specific intervals. Honey, wooden planks, and copal were due every eighty days. Cloaks, other garments, and copper had to be sent every six months, while one year was allowed for producing war dresses, shields, paper, bins of grain, gold, and turquoise.

Book Two of the *Florentine Codex*, an Aztec book compiled under the direction of Spanish priest Bernardino de Sahagún, contains lists of tribute required from the towns. A column of pictographs identifying the towns appears on each page. Other pictographs illustrate the items to be sent, such as grain bins, bowls, shields, and tunics. Above the tribute symbols are more pictographs indicating the quantity of each item to be sent. The Aztecs "used a base-20 number system for arithmetic, calendrics, and land measurement," Smith explains. "This numbering system was also used for commerce and tribute since goods were measured by counts and volume, not by weight. . . . There were glyphs for quantities of 1, 20, 400, and 8,000."[19] For instance, in the Aztec tribute lists, a flag glyph equals 20, a feather equals 400 (20 x 20), and a tasseled flag equals 8,000 (20 x 400). If 800 mantles are required as tribute, for example, two feathers appear above a pictograph of the mantle.

Careful attention to tribute was vital for the well-being of city-state rulers and their subjects. Nothing short of outright rebellion could bring down the wrath of the supreme powers at Tenochtitlán like failure to send the proper tribute at the appointed times. Since it was the common people who actually produced the items, responsibility ultimately lay with them. In this manner, tribute served not only to enrich the empire, but also to keep the common people too busy to think about rebellion.

Subjugated City-States

In addition to the core city-states, the Aztecs eventually controlled over four hundred other small territories and exacted tribute from them as well. For example, many products highly prized by the Aztecs (such as cacao beans from which chocolate was made, feathers from tropical birds, and cotton fibers) came only from the warm, low-lying states outside the core of the empire. Consequently, these states were prime targets for Aztec military campaigns, and many of these regions were subjugated for strictly economic purposes.

Like the core city-states, subjugated territories were allowed to govern themselves as long as they lived up to the tribute demands made of them. Those located on the borders of the empire were sometimes exempted from sending large amounts of tribute in return for protecting the flanks of the empire against enemies of the Aztecs.

From the Aztec city-states as well as from conquered territories, tons of tribute goods flowed daily into the city of Tenochtitlan on the backs of porters and in the holds of canoes. The empire was rich and it was orderly. Laws were severe and punishment for wrongdoers was swift and sure.

Aztec Law

Aztec law at the height of the empire was a complex system with higher and lower courts, judges, and attorneys. An Aztec leader closely associated with the development of the legal system was Nezahualcoyotl, an influential ruler of the Triple Alliance. In order to consolidate the many small kingdoms within the growing empire, Nezahualcoyotl imposed a system of eighty laws on all the regions.

Even though the laws were strict and punishments harsh, the Aztec court system had certain features that guaranteed fairness regardless of gender or social class. A person accused of a crime could be represented by an attorney, present witnesses and testimony, and appeal an unfavorable decision to a higher court. Although women did not enjoy equality with men under the law, they could own property, make legal contracts, and sue in the courts. In the matter of adultery, both men and women received the same punishment.

Members of the nobility who committed crimes were often punished more severely than commoners because they were supposed to be models of moral behavior for the common classes. Archaeologist Warwick Bray writes:

A drunken official or priest was executed, but if the offender was a common man, he got away more lightly. On the first occasion his head was shaved in public and his house knocked down, but if he were unlucky enough to be caught a second time the penalty was death. Even the ruler's family was bound by the law, and Nezahualcoyotl had three of his sons executed for violating the code he had drawn up.[20]

As the empire grew in size and power, laws became increasingly standardized, with little regard for extenuating circumstances. In practice, however, the severity of the formal law was often moderated. Townsend explains that "not everything could actually be judged in a strictly 'legalistic' manner. Indeed, there was an entirely different aspect of justice centered on the concept of 'the reasonable man,' under which there were no rigid prescriptions for crime and punishment but judgments were instead made according to general, culturally accepted notions of reasonable behavior."[21]

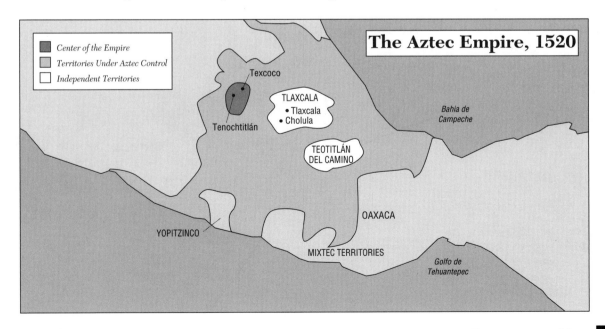

The Aztec Empire, 1520

Center of the Empire
Territories Under Aztec Control
Independent Territories

Texcoco
TLAXCALA
• Tlaxcala
• Cholula
Tenochtitlán
Bahia de Campeche
TEOTITLÁN DEL CAMINO
OAXACA
YOPITZINCO
MIXTEC TERRITORIES
Golfo de Tehuantepec

Even Nezahualcoyotl's penal code had reasonable features. For instance, stealing corn was a serious crime, but a hungry person was permitted to pluck corn from a few rows that were planted by the roadsides just for that purpose.

Aztec Judicial System

A system of courts existed throughout the Aztec Empire, with the common courts at the local level and appeals courts higher up the line. In the local courts, men from the common classes who had distinguished themselves as warriors or community leaders were appointed as judges. At this level, they could make decisions only about petty crimes. More serious crimes were investigated at the local level, but the accused was sent to the next level for disposition of his or her case. These higher courts were located in the capitals of each city-state as well as at Tenochtitlán, and the judges were members of the nobility.

If the accused was a noble or if the matter was legally complicated, the case could be appealed to the next level, which met in Tenochtitlán in the emperor's palace. The judges at this court were distinguished members of the nobility. After that, there was only

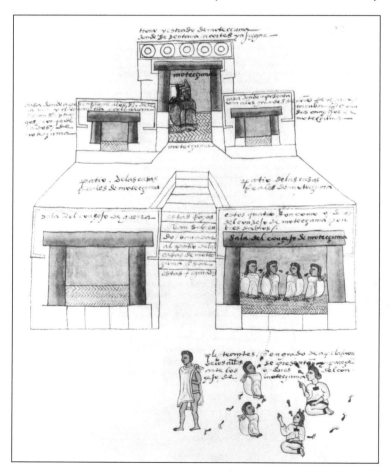

This illustration shows Montezuma seated on his throne in his palace with his judicial council seated below. The emperor's judicial council was the highest court in Aztec society.

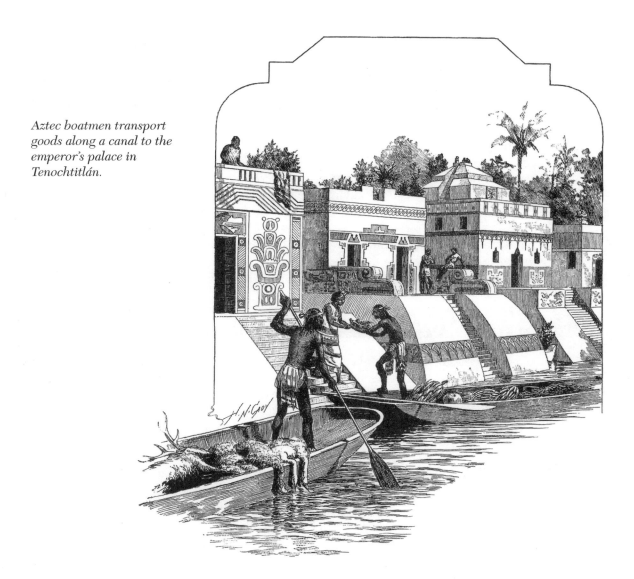

Aztec boatmen transport goods along a canal to the emperor's palace in Tenochtitlán.

one appeal left—to the emperor himself, who held court every ten days or so in the palace.

At the emperor's court, the petitioner stated his case to the emperor and his panel of legal advisers. After considering the matter, the advisers gave their opinions to the emperor, who then made the decision. Once the emperor had spoken, there was no further appeal. Díaz del Castillo writes in his memoirs, "Thereupon the litigants said no more but retired without turning their backs, and after making the customary three bows, went out into the hall."[22]

Judges at all levels were appointed to their positions and held accountable for their behavior. Because they were supposed to set a good example, corrupt judges were subject to stiff punishments themselves. A page in an Aztec codex shows a judge being strangled for accepting a bribe.

Aztec Punishments

The ideal citizen in Aztec society was self-disciplined, honest, industrious, and fiercely loyal to the family, community, and emperor. Consequently, the harshest laws were reserved for violations of those principles. Drunkenness, adultery, theft, and rebellion all carried severe penalties, frequently death. The Aztec attitude toward drunkards, for instance, is described in the *Florentine Codex* as follows:

> They [the Aztecs] also say that to no purpose is the drunkard; no longer doth he know what he sayeth, what he divulgeth.

Nothing tranquil, nothing peaceful cometh from his mouth. The pulque [fermented cactus juice] completely harmeth, completely ruineth humanity, the character of things; [so] the old men went saying. . . . "For this reason the lords, the rulers who acted for the realm, who gave forth the word of our lord, go stoning people on account of pulque; they go hanging people because of it.[23]

Seemingly harmless behaviors that violated the Aztec dress code carried severe penalties as well, either because they showed disregard for the emperor or because they blurred the

Tlacaelel: A Powerful Noble

One of the most interesting and powerful leaders in Aztec history was not an emperor, but an adviser to emperors. His name was Tlacaelel, half-brother of Aztec emperor Montezuma I. His tremendous influence on the formation and expansion of the Aztec Empire as well as his role in the increase of human sacrifice are discussed in this excerpt from *Mesoweb: An Exploration of Mesoamerican Cultures*. The ideas expressed on the website are based on the book *Aztec Thought and Culture* by Miguel Léon-Portilla.

"A significant figure in the rise of the Aztec state was . . . Tlacaelel. [He] was born on the same day as the emperor Motecuhzoma the Great. They had the same father but different mothers. Though he turned down the opportunity to become emperor himself, Tlacaelel went on to serve three rulers as prime minister. . . . He first emerges in the annals of history during an important crisis in the early years of [the Aztec rise to power].

Having spent the latter part of their migration being driven to and fro by more settled peoples, the Aztecs were now threatened by subjugation to the neighboring Tepanecs. [The weary Aztec were ready to surrender to the Tepanecs, but Tlacaelel protested.] 'Let us go forward and fight the Tepanecs as duty and honor demand,' he proposed. 'If we fail in the attempt, cut us up and make a good meal of us.' The Tepanecs were decisively defeated, and in the afterglow of this success, Tlacaelel set out to instill in the Aztecs a sense that they were a chosen people, whose role was to conquer and dominate. The Aztec's tribal god Huitzilopochtli was both their god of the sun and of war. [Huitzilopochtli's] declaration to his wandering people at the time of their great migration that he, their guardian deity and inspiration, was born for conquest may well have been inserted into the legend at this time. For it was Tlacaelel who added the nuance [suggestion] that the Aztecs' imperial mission had as its basis the necessity of providing sacrificial blood for the nourishment of the Sun."

all-important distinction between the common people and the nobility.

Corporal punishments included jailing, beating, stoning, strangulation, and burning. Jails were constituted of wooden cages in which prisoners were kept on public display before going on trial or being executed. Long-term imprisonment was not used as punishment. Stoning was accomplished by crushing the condemned person's head with a stone ax. Strangulation meant having a rope looped around the neck while an executioner on either side of the prisoner pulled on the ends of the rope. Fines and restitution were applied to property crimes. Sometimes guilty persons were sentenced to become slaves to their victims until the debt was repaid.

Emperors and Punishment

Emperors sometimes created their own laws and penalties on the spot when something displeased them. For example, after Montezuma II's warriors lost an important battle, he commanded that their heads be shaved and their elaborate battle dresses and insignia destroyed. Since a warrior's clothing and hairstyle signified his rank and accomplishments, this punishment was personally devastating. Even those who had to carry out the sentences were sad and distressed. In his history of the Aztecs, Spanish priest Diego Duran tells of the sorrow that followed:

> With great sadness, with sorrow, the justices, who had no alternative, carried out the sentence and commands of their king. . . . The justices returned from having performed their duties and informed the king of the weeping and sadness that

these actions had caused, and how the city seemed empty and lonely with the captains and lords locked up in their houses, not daring to go out. There was no one in the streets, no one enjoying himself, no one enlivening the city as was customary. But the king showed no regret, no sorrow, but rather feigned indifference and ignored the soldiers all that year, treating them as despicable men of low birth who should be disgraced.[24]

On another occasion, Montezuma's astrologers and seers failed to observe an unusual object in the sky, perhaps a comet. When Montezuma heard of the sighting from other sources, he was furious and probably deeply troubled as well. Celestial sightings such as this were often taken as omens of future disasters. He therefore called his nobles together to express his displeasure and punish the offenders. He commanded that all of his astrologers and seers be dragged through the streets and killed because they had failed in their duties. In addition, he decreed that all their possessions should be taken from them, their houses destroyed, and their wives and children sold into slavery. "This was the terribly cruel punishment that [Montezuma] gave to anyone who failed to conform to his demands, who did not carry out his orders," writes Duran. "Therefore he was feared and obeyed with such diligence and care that everything ran smoothly, to the minutest detail."[25]

Even though the emperor behaved harshly when displeased, the Aztec justice system itself was fair and impartial. Law was necessary and important, but in Aztec thinking, an even better way to create a well-ordered society was by educating the children to be brave, honest, and dedicated to the empire and its gods.

Education and Communication

Aztec children were trained for adult roles at home by their parents and other family members until their early teens. After that, they were sent to free schools where training for their adult roles continued and other types of studies began. Aztec parents considered their children's education very important. While still infants, children were formally enrolled in the schools they would later attend. Schools for girls and boys were strictly separated, and schools for commoners were separated from those for the nobility.

All Aztec schools emphasized oral communication because Nahuatl, the Aztec language, was not written down phonetically until after the Spanish conquest in the sixteenth century. In addition to their spoken language, the Aztecs used a system of hieroglyphic or picture writing. Specially trained scribes recorded many kinds of information in handmade folding books. Because these books were costly and required special training to read, they were used only in schools for children of the nobility.

In addition to communication taught in the schools, another vitally important kind of communication for the Aztecs was a human messenger system that linked the extensive empire from one end to the other.

Schools for Children of the Common Class

Each neighborhood (*calpulli*) in Aztec towns and cities was obliged to provide schools for the common children of the district. Aztec schools were called *telpochcalli*, which means "youth house." Boys actually lived at school, where their primary task was learning to become warriors. The Aztecs did not keep a standing army so every male had to be ready to fight when called upon. "Training in matters of war was primarily entrusted to the war captains and trainers," writes anthropologist Ross Hassig. "When an instructing warrior went to war, he took a youth as an apprentice to carry his supplies and arms. Many youths sought to become warriors, though life in the *telpochcalli* was spartan."[26]

Boys in the *telpochcalli* were subject to stern discipline and hard work. They kept the school clean and did manual labor in the community, such as making adobe bricks or cleaning out canals. Boys also were instructed in rhetoric and speech, as there were no books or writing in the common schools. Thus, the ability to memorize passages and to speak effectively was a very important part of the curriculum. In Aztec society, an educated person was one who could express his or her thoughts clearly as well as quote traditional passages from Aztec literature, poetry, and song. "To be educated was to be a master of expression," historian Richard Townsend comments. "An educated person had to be able to make artful or moving speeches on a diversity of occasions with all the etiquette prescribed by the ritualized pattern of Aztec life."[27]

Cuicacalli—House of Song

Details about *telpochcalli* schools for girls are not as well known, but Aztec girls of the common classes were involved in the study of religious rituals and traditional music and dancing. These classes were held in a special area of the temple called a *cuicacalli* or "house of song." These classes also included boys because everyone in Aztec society learned to sing and dance, accompanied by flutes and percussion instruments.

Drums and gongs were used to set the rhythm for dancing and singing. Drums were made from hollow logs with animal skin or snakeskin stretched over the top. Small drums were played with the hands. Gongs, which produced a higher pitch than drums, were made of small, hollowed-out logs with closed ends. They were laid horizontally on stands and played with rubber-tipped mallets. Grooves cut in the top and bottom provided different tones when the gongs were struck. Bells and rattles of various types provided other rhythmic sounds.

Melodies were played on pottery flutes that could sound about five tones, but no one today knows how the melodies sounded. The words of many Aztec songs and poems are known, however, because they were passed down orally through generations. A poem written by Nezahualcoyotl, king of Texcoco, expresses this thought:

My flowers shall not cease to live;
My songs shall never end:
I, the singer, intone them;
they become scattered,
they are spread about.[28]

The houses of song provided a psychological release from the tightly controlled social system with its emphasis on separation of the sexes. Singing and dancing also

---

The *Cuicacalli* or "House of Song": A Social Leveler in a Stratified Society

The gulf between the nobility and the common people in Aztec society was wide and deep. One experience that united Aztecs of all social classes, however, was participation in activities at the "house of song." In the following excerpt from *The Aztecs*, archaeologist Brian M. Fagan describes what took place at the *cuicacalli* and how those activities cut across social class barriers.

"The time spent in the *cuicacalli*, the 'House of Song,' was a critical period in Aztec education, for here everyone, noble and commoner, went through a highly structured curriculum of singing, dancing, and music.

Each *calpulli* had its own *cuicacalli* where elderly men and women assembled the students an hour before sunset for long sessions of dancing and recitation. Here everyone, however humble, learned the correct songs and orations for every major religious ceremony on the Aztec calendar. These incantations spoke of the Aztec cosmos, the creation, and the great migrations of the ancestors. They dealt with the roles of mortals on earth, and of the relationships between gods and humans. At the *cuicacalli* everyone learned about their cultural heritage and about the mystical and highly symbolic world that surrounded them."

provided a means of passing down and reinforcing the history, traditions, and values of the Aztec people. For a people without a written language, this was especially important.

Schools for Children of the Elite Class

Schools for children of the ruling class, called *calmecac* schools, were fewer in number because the nobility made up only a tiny portion of the population. *Calmecac* schools were associated with temples in towns and cities and were separated by gender like the common schools. *Calmecac* schools for boys were similar to common schools in that the students lived at the school and were trained in warfare. In matters of discipline and physical labor, *calmecac* schools probably were even stricter than common schools. In his book *Everyday Life of the Aztecs*, archaeologist Warwick Bray describes a noble boy's life at a *calmecac* school:

> The curriculum laid emphasis on self-control, humility, and unselfishness, for the teachers believed that those who were to lead must first learn to obey. . . . Although the youths were mostly of high birth they were given menial tasks to do, like cleaning and sweeping, or farm work on the temple lands, or the collection of firewood in the hills. They were made to fast and do penance going alone at night to deserted places in the mountains . . . where they offered incense and mortified their flesh by drawing blood from their ears and legs with maguey spines. At midnight all the boys were roused from their beds to pray and to take a cold bath in the pool.[29]

The major difference between the two types of boys' schools was their overall purpose. *Calmecac* schools served as academies of higher learning where the sons of the nobility were prepared for the high offices they would eventually hold. In addition to warrior training, *calmecac* boys were instructed in academic subjects such as writing, religion, law, and science. Occasionally, outstanding young men from the common classes were allowed to attend these schools.

At the *calmecac* schools for girls, the daughters of the nobility were trained to manage the households of their future spouses. This did not mean the training was soft or easy. Girls were subject to firm discipline and were expected to be models of virtue. Like their common class "sisters," elite girls learned to spin and weave and were given instruction in religion, morality, history, and tradition.

Schools for the Priesthood

Another educational option for students was the priesthood. This avenue was open to boys and girls of all classes, but the top levels of the priesthood were reserved for the nobility. Parents dedicated their children to the priesthood while they were still infants in traditional ceremonies involving many long speeches from the parents and Aztec priests. Parents accepted certain responsibilities toward the upkeep of the temple as their part of the bargain. In early adolescence, children who were thus dedicated to the priesthood entered school, where life was both mentally and physically challenging. This was particularly true for boys. Historian Richard Townsend describes the duties of a male student priest: "Meditation and the learning of prayers were accompanied by periods of fasting," he writes. "Long vigils were kept and ac-

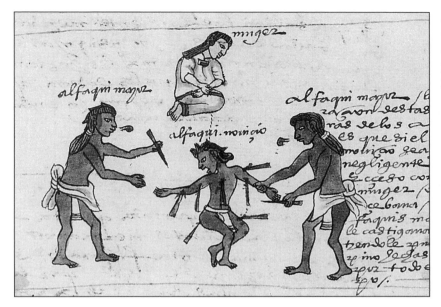

Aztec boys studying for the priesthood were subject to grueling physical trials. Here, priests repeatedly stab a novice with cactus spines in a ritual bloodletting ceremony.

companied by periodic offerings and purifying baths; food was usually taken in meager amounts at midday and midnight. Special occasions demanded auto-sacrifice; blood would be drawn by pricking the legs and arms with maguey [cactus] spines, by cutting the earlobes with obsidian blades or by running a cord through the tongue."[30]

Young women who entered the priesthood were trained to carry out the less prominent, but essential roles assigned to women in Aztec religious observances. Most of these roles had to do with honoring earth goddesses and other female deities. Priestesses also served as teachers in schools for girls. Women were allowed to leave the priesthood to marry if their parents and temple authorities agreed, and many of them did.

The men in the priesthood were expected to remain unmarried and celibate, but a variety of careers within the priesthood were open to them. Depending upon his interests and abilities, a priest might become a teacher, a codex painter and scribe, an astrologer, or even a warrior.

Spoken Language and "Written" Communication

A majority of the Aztec people spoke Nahuatl, a language belonging to the Uto-Aztecan family of languages. Linguists call it an agglutinating language, meaning that a host of prefixes and suffixes may be attached to a root word to indicate such things as tense, gender, and location. For example, the Nahuatl word *simosepantasohtakan* (you shall love each other) is made up of the Aztec words *si* (you shall), *mo* (each other), *sepan* (altogether), *tasohta* (love), *kan* (indicates plurality or "you" in the plural form). In an empire made up of many diverse groups, a common language was an important unifying factor. In all Aztec schools, stress was placed on learning Aztec history, customs, and traditions through memorization and repetition, often to the accompaniment of drums.

Some of the privileged and scholarly Aztec people also communicated through picture writing, which was made up of five types of symbols—pictographs, ideograms, phonograms, number symbols, and calendar symbols. Pictographs are drawings of objects that represent the real thing—a picture of a temple means a temple. An ideogram is a drawing that represents not the object pictured but a related idea. In Aztec picture writing, for example, a broken temple with fire coming from it is an ideogram. When an army invaded, it captured and set fire to the enemy's temple. Thus a picture of a burning temple came to mean "conquest." A phonogram is a symbol that represents a word, syllable, or single speech sound. Historian Mario Araujo explains:

> Every word in spoken language has a sound as well as a meaning, and glyphs were sometimes used to indicate the pho-

netic value of a word rather than its sense. Thus, to give an example from English, a drawing of an eye may be a pictogram (meaning the eye as part of the body), or an ideogram (expressing the idea of sight and vision), or a phonogram (standing for the sound "I"). In the latter case, the eye symbol can be used, as a sort of pun, to indicate the first person singular. . . . The Aztecs applied the same technique to the writing of Nahuatl. Pictures were sometimes used for their sound, without reference to their meaning.[31]

Although it had limits, Aztec picture writing was used to record historical events, cultural traditions, laws, governmental records, and business matters. The information to be conveyed

Although the Nahuatl language lacked an alphabet, scholarly Aztecs communicated in writing using ideograms, like those seen here, and other symbols.

was painted on long strips of handmade paper and folded accordion-style into books.

Aztec Books

In one of his letters to the Spanish king, Cortés expressed his amazement at the thousands of these folded books he saw in the palace of the emperor. Bernal Díaz del Castillo, a soldier in Cortés's army, also mentions these books in his memoirs. Writing about one of Montezuma's stewards, Bernal Díaz del Castillo said, "he kept an account of all the revenue that was brought to Montezuma in his books, which were made of paper—their name for which is *amal*—and he had a great house full of these books."[32]

The paper mentioned by Bernal Díaz del Castillo was made from the inner bark of wild fig trees. A lot of this paper was made in Morelos, a region south of Tenochtitlán where fig trees grew abundantly. Papermaking was an important industry in Morelos, and the production included many steps—stripping the bark, removing the sap, loosening the fibers by boiling, beating the fibers with stone hammers to fuse them, and finally coating them with a white lime mixture. Using paints made from natural pigments, specially trained scribes painted pictures and symbols on both sides of long paper strips. When completed, the books were folded accordion-style so that both sides could be viewed. Books were a privilege reserved for the nobility, and only a few high-placed officials or priests within that select group were able to read and interpret them.

Preserving Aztec Picture Writing

Thousands of Aztec books were destroyed by the Spaniards during and after the conquest

Nahuatl Pronunciation

About a million people in Mexico today still speak Nahuatl, the language of the Aztecs, or at least modern dialects of it. Nahuatl was not a written language until Spanish missionaries transliterated it into the Spanish alphabet in the sixteenth century. Although the written words appear strange to English speakers, a few rules help in pronouncing them. Archaeologist Brian M. Fagan offers some common phonetic values from his book *The Aztecs*.

cu as in *Culhuacan*, is pronounced *koo* (as in *cool*)

ch is pronounced *tch* (as in *ch*urch)

c before *a* or *o* is pronounced as *k* (as in *cave*)

c before *e* or *i* is an *s* sound (as in *save*)

h is pronounced with a soft aspiration as it is in English

hu is sounded as *w* (as in *we*)

q is only found in the constructions *qua*, *que*, and *qui*, where it is pronounced *ka*, *ke*, *ki*

tl, *ts*, and *tz* represent single sounds (as in spo*ts*) and should not be divided

u before *a*, *e*, *i*, and *o* is pronounced like the English *w*

x is always pronounced as *sh* (as in *sh*eet)

z before *e* and *i* is an *s* sound (as in mi*ss*)

in order to eradicate the old order and establish a new society. However, soon after the conquest, both Aztec and Spanish scholars went to great lengths to rescue Aztec picture writing before it was lost forever. One of these

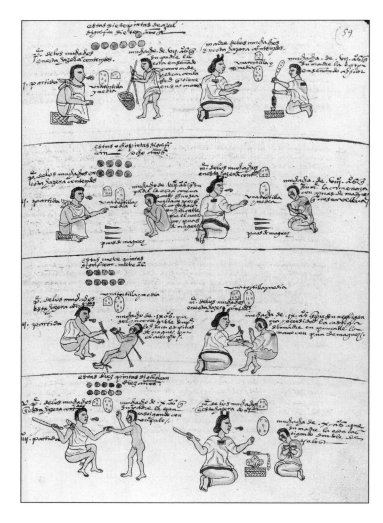

Compiled shortly after the Spanish conquest, the Codex Mendoza *provides a pictorial history of the Aztecs. The section shown here illustrates elders teaching children.*

was a Spanish priest, Bernardino de Sahagún, who spent years collecting information from the Aztecs themselves. He then employed Aztec scribes to re-create traditional books based on the information he gathered. Sahagún's work, known as *The General History of the Things of New Spain*, or the *Florentine Codex*, is one of the most valuable sources of Aztec history and culture. Another valuable source is the *Codex Mendoza*, compiled soon after the conquest and illustrated by Aztec artists. It contains a pictorial history of Aztec rulers and their conquests, records of tribute required from cities and towns of the empire, and the life cycle of an Aztec citizen from birth to death.

Lines of Communication Among the Aztec City-States

Before Europeans arrived in the Valley of Mexico, communicating the spoken and written word to the various city-states of the empire was carried out by *titlantil*, messengers who traveled on foot and worked in relays.

Messenger stations on the main roads were two leagues apart, which equals about eight-and-a-half kilometers or a little over five miles. Rulers and other officials sent messengers for many different purposes. However, messengers were especially important in times of war for sending instructions to military commanders and relaying news of the battles back to the home cities and towns. Anthropologist Peter Nabokov describes the *titlantil:*

> Spanish writers refer to the seasoned runners among the Aztec of Mexico [as those] "who could run like the wind." Ceremonially they served to disperse fire from a sacred flame periodically rekindled in a central temple; functionally, they moved in relays to convey messages. *Correos* in Spanish, *titlantil* to the Aztec, they were valued for veracity as well as strength. The historian William H. Prescott says that these men, "trained from childhood," covered one to two hundred miles a day [in relays], bearing hides covered with hieroglyphic writing. Hernan Cortes wrote that within twenty-four hours of his landing at Chianiztlan in May 1519, runners had described to Montezuma, 260 miles away, his ships, men, guns and horses.[33]

There was also an informal system of spreading news. In his memoirs, Bernal Díaz del Castillo tells about a group of Montezuma's tax collectors who came into a village where conquistador Cortés and his men were camping. As representatives of the emperor, the tax collectors haughtily demanded tribute from the villagers. Their attitude irritated Cortés, who quietly called the village headman aside and demanded that he arrest the tax collectors and jail them. The headman was terrified of defying the emperor, but Cortés said that he and his army would protect the

An Aztec Poet-Philosopher

Nezahualcoyotl, whose name means "hungry coyote," was a remarkable ruler of Texcoco, one of the regions in the Aztec Triple Alliance. He was famous not only as a great warrior and political leader, but as a poet and philosopher as well. The following poem attributed to him is quoted in *Moctezuma's Mexico* by David Carrasco and Eduardo Matos Moctezuma.

> I comprehend the secret,
>   the hidden:
> O my lords!
> Thus we are,
> we are mortal,
> men through and through
> we all will have to go away,
> we all will have to die on earth.
> Like a painting,
> we will be erased.
> Like a flower,
> we will dry up
> here on earth . . .
> Think on this my lords,
> eagles and ocelots,
> though you be of jade,
> though you be of gold
> you also will go there
> to the place of the fleshless.

headman from Montezuma's wrath. The headman accordingly did as Cortés wished. "So the news spread throughout the province," Díaz del Castillo writes, "for the . . . [headman] immediately sent messengers to proclaim it, and the chiefs who had accompanied the tax-gatherers scattered immediately after the arrest, each to his own town, to convey the order and give an account of what had happened."[34]

The Work of Father Bernardino de Sahagún

Modern historical research cannot surpass the work of Father Bernardino de Sahagún, a Spanish priest in Mexico almost five hundred years ago. His diligence in saving the history and culture of the Aztec is summarized in this excerpt from *The Aztec Image of Self and Society* by Miguel Léon-Portilla. Sahagún's masterwork, called *The General History of the Things of New Spain,* or *Florentine Codex,* is owned by the Lorenzo Medici Library in Florence, Italy.

"Sahagun, having arrived in Mexico in 1529, devoted himself as no one else to the study of the cultural institutions of the precontact world. In his attempt to penetrate into the native consciousness, he drew up questionnaires to address all the points he was interested in investigating. Among other themes, he included questions about the rites, priests, gods, feasts, customs, the heavens, the count of the years, the hereafter, human affairs, kinship, customs of the lords, occupations, insignia, legends, formal education, child-rearing practices, sexual morals, astrology, the crafts, intellectuals, philosophical ideas, law, medicine, nutrition, botany, animals, precious metals, stones, ethnic origins, literature, proverbs, refrains, moral and theological discourses, hymns and songs, and even a native version of the history of the conquest.

In order to obtain information in the Nahuatl language . . . Sahagun sought out . . . indigenous elders who knew their traditions and who, with the aid of pictures, could inform him about the diverse subjects he sought to record. In addition, various students from the Indian College of Santa Cruz in Tlateloco, disciples of Fray Bernardino, provided him with invaluable assistance. . . . In this way, Sahagun compiled hundreds of folios in which are included pictures of and Nahuatl texts on almost every aspect of precontact Nahua culture and the physical environment that framed it."

Role of Communication

These two types of communication provided a large measure of stability for the Aztec empire. The first, passing down social and cultural principles in free schools by means of language and symbols, made all Aztec citizens acutely aware of their place in society and what was expected of them. The second type, long-distance communication by human messengers, allowed Aztec leaders to integrate and govern a diverse and extensive empire.

These tightly planned and regulated systems did not stifle the creativity of the Aztec, however, for some of the finest examples of architecture, arts, and crafts in ancient America were produced by Aztec builders and artisans.

CHAPTER 4

Architecture, Arts, and Crafts

Although Aztec architects and artisans relied heavily upon traditional themes and skills of earlier Mesoamerican societies, goldsmiths, weavers, feather workers, and stone sculptors added innovative and original touches to their works. The same is true for Aztec architects and builders who moved beyond tradition to create new forms and styles. When the Aztecs began rebuilding their capital city at Tenochtitlán in the fifteenth century, they adopted many of the architectural features of Tenochtitlán. This once-powerful city located thirty-one miles northeast of Tenochtitlán, had collapsed three centuries or more before the Aztecs came to the Valley of Mexico. The ruined city was revered by the Aztecs as the birthplace of the gods and thus served as a model for the reconstruction of Tenochtitlán.

However, the Aztecs added their own architectural features to traditional designs. One of these was placing two temples at the top of the great pyramid rather than the traditional single temple. Other distinctive architectural features in the sacred precinct were the spaciousness of the buildings and the great number of structures that were clustered together—no less than seventy-eight structures including temples, towers, monuments, priests' residences, and ball courts. A high wall with a gate on each of its four sides enclosed the sacred precinct. Government buildings and the palaces of the emperor and other high officials were located just outside the wall.

Although other urban areas of the empire were not as splendid or as well planned as Tenochtitlán, all Aztec cities included a sacred precinct at the center. Without exception, the most prominent feature in the sacred precinct of every city was the temple.

Aztec Temples

The most familiar feature of Aztec architecture is the temple—a flat-topped pyramid with steps leading up one side and one or two small shrines at the top. This general plan had many variations, depending upon where the pyramid was located and the types of building materials that were available. The interior of most pyramids was filled with earth or rubble and the exterior was overlaid with stone or adobe bricks. Some pyramids were terraced like a series of small platforms placed on top of each other. Occasionally small rooms were recessed in the terrace walls. Over time, many temples were enlarged by building new facades over old structures.

Although the ruins of Aztec temples are still impressive, in their days of glory they were spectacular. Some temples had whitewashed walls while others were painted in many vivid colors. Temples were also decorated with colorful frescoes, statues of the gods in their many guises, and decorative accents skillfully carved in stone.

Aztec Palaces

The palaces where kings and nobles lived were always located near the temples to impress commoners with the close relationship between their rulers and the gods. Palaces and civic buildings where people actually lived and worked had to be accessible and spacious, so the architectural style of these structures was completely different from the temples.

Doorways and other openings in palaces were supported with post and lintel construction or corbelled arches. Post and lintel construction uses two vertical columns of the same height with a horizontal beam of wood or stone laid across the top. A corbelled arch is made by extending each row of building blocks inward on both sides of an opening until they meet at the top. The result is a triangular doorway with opposite sides of the triangle bulging outward slightly. The Aztecs,

The Aztecs obtained much of their architectural inspiration from the anient ruins of Teotihuacan, a city buiilt by unknown peoples long before the Aztec empire was founded.

as well as all other Mesoamerican societies, were unaware of the Roman or keystone arch, which is capable of supporting greater weight. Because of this architectural limitation, Aztec palaces and civic buildings were never more than two stories high.

Whatever Aztec palaces lacked in height, however, they more than made up for in horizontal spaciousness. When Cortés and his army arrived at Tenochtitlán in November 1519, Emperor Montezuma met them at the gates and invited them into the city. In his memoirs, Spanish soldier Bernal Díaz del Castillo remembers that day. He writes, "They led us to our quarters which were in some large houses capable of accommodating us all and had formerly belonged to the great Montezuma's father."[35] Considering that Cortés's army consisted of four hundred men, their equipment, and a large number of horses, the palace must have been quite large indeed.

Homes of the Common People

Of course, only kings lived like kings. Living quarters for the lesser nobility were not as lavish as those higher up the scale, and the quality of commoners' dwellings decreased appreciably from high to low classes. In large

Architecture, Arts, and Crafts **47**

cities, common people lived and worked in flat-topped apartment complexes around an open courtyard. An extended family or perhaps a group of artisans would share such a complex. Home furnishings were sparse, consisting mainly of storage chests, baskets, and reed mats for sitting and sleeping. In the kitchen, tortillas were baked on an earthenware griddle that was balanced on three large stones above a hearth.

The living quarters of commoners in towns and villages followed the same general arrangement. However, in the countryside, houses were more likely to be single-family dwellings made of wattle and daub (mud plastered over a framework of branches).

Aztec Artisans

Archaeological excavations reveal that many Aztec families produced craft items for the market as well as for their own use. Almost all families in the common classes worked at crafts at least part of the time to supply their family's own needs, to fulfill tribute quotas, and to trade for other goods. Because the production of luxury goods (such as gold and feather work) required expensive raw materials and special skills, those items became the specialties of trained artisans who passed the skills on to their children. Most of the artisans who produced luxury goods were commoners. Although they could not become nobles,

The Art of Feather Working

Feather workers were highly regarded in Aztec society for their skill in transforming objects and clothing into marvelous works of art using the plumage from birds of many species. Producing a feathered object or garment was a complex project that occupied an entire family. In this excerpt from *Everyday Life of the Aztecs*, author and archaeologist Warwick Bray describes the many steps required in this unusual art form.

"Making a feather mosaic was a complicated process. First the scribe painted the design, full size, on a sheet of paper, then the craftsman made a stencil or template from the pattern. . . . This stencil was used to transfer the design onto a sheet of cotton backed with maguey, and the worker was now ready to apply the first layer of feathers. Since these would be invisible in the finished article he used the cheaper kind of plumage, some of it dyed to the requisite colour. The feathers were trimmed with a cop-

per knife on a cutting board, dipped into glue, and applied, one by one, with a bone spatula to the cloth, first the outlines in black, then the main parts of the design. . . . The final layer was applied in the same manner as the first, but this time the workman used precious feathers—green quetzal plumes, eagle down, and the brightly coloured plumage of the cotinga (blue), roseate spoonbill (red), parrot (yellow), and hummingbird (turquoise).

All members of the family helped with the work. The men prepared the stencils and did the cutting and mounting, while the children who were learning the trade prepared the glue from bat excrement or pulverized roots, and the women dyed and sorted the feathers. No glue was used in the manufacture of mantles and headdresses. Instead the quills were individually knotted or sewn on to a backing, consisting either of a wooden framework or, in case of cloaks and tunics, a flexible woven material."

they did enjoy high status within the common class. According to art historian Elizabeth Hill Boone,

> They were gold workers, coppercasters, lapidaries [artisans who worked with gemstones], turquoise-mosaic workers, feather workers, specialist weavers, and producers of rabbit-fur garments and cloth. Most of these artisans were drawn to the cities, where they produced goods for the rulers and nobility. Their products were items of clothing, personal ornaments, and costumes for war and religious celebrations. They either worked directly in the rulers' households or worked independently on commission.[36]

Specialists lived in their own residential sectors in the cities and often had guilds to support their interests. There was even a social hierarchy among artisans, of which the most prestigious were the feather workers.

Feather Workers

The *amanteca,* or feather workers, were almost as high in social rank as the long-distance merchants, who were richer than some members of the nobility. The two groups even lived near each other in a mutually beneficial relationship. Feather workers depended upon merchants to bring exotic feathers from the far corners of the empire, which, in turn, provided a steady market for the merchants.

The most highly prized feathers came from tropical birds with bright plumage, such as the colorful quetzal bird with its long tail feathers, the blue cotinga, and the roseate spoonbill. Feathers were used to make headdresses, ceremonial costumes, ornaments, standards (ceremonial banners), shields,

cloaks, and other clothing. Different methods were used to attach the feathers. They were glued on inflexible objects such as shields, but tied into place on clothing and other fabrics.

When Spanish conquistador Hernán Cortés suddenly appeared in Mexico, Aztec emperor Montezuma presented him with many gifts. Among them was a spectacular headdress made of five hundred bright green tail feathers of the quetzal bird and decorated with gold disks and smaller feathers of red and blue. Cortés later sent the headdress to King Charles V of Spain, who also was the archduke of Austria. The headdress, forty-six inches high and still retaining its vivid colors, is currently displayed in the Museum of Ethnology in Vienna, Austria.

Stone Sculptors

The Aztecs produced extremely talented, but anonymous stone sculptors whose monumental works were discovered long after the conquest of the Aztecs in 1521. One of these works is an immense stone disk intricately carved with Aztec symbols. It was discovered in the late seventeenth century by workers who were making repairs in Mexico City where the great Aztec temple formerly stood. The huge disk, called the sunstone, is twelve feet in diameter, three feet thick, and weighs twenty-five tons. Faint traces of color on it show that it had once been painted in many brilliant colors. When the stone was first discovered, it was thought to be a calendar. However, further study revealed that the carvings on it depict the Aztec view of the cosmos, with the face of the sun god in the center.

In 1790, a statue of the Aztec earth goddess, Coatlicue, was found in the same general area. Sculpted by a master artisan, the

Aztec feather workers created elaborate ceremonial shields shown in this illustration of Montezuma I.

goddess's head is formed of two serpents and her feet are huge claws like those of an eagle. She wears a skirt of entwined snakes and a necklace on which hang a skull and severed human hearts and hands.

A more recent discovery in 1978 is another large stone disk depicting the death of the moon goddess, Coyolxauhqui. In Aztec mythology, Coyolxauhqui was the sister of Huitzilopochtli, the patron god of the Aztecs. She and her other brothers sought to kill their mother, who was pregnant with Huitzilopochtli. At the crucial moment, however, Huitzilopochtli was born full-grown, wearing a suit of armor, and brandishing weapons. He cut off his sister's head and she fell down a hill. When she hit the bottom, her body broke apart. The relief carving on the stone, which is almost eleven feet across, shows Coyolxauhqui lying on the ground with her severed head and limbs positioned around her.

Aztec stone carvers also made smaller, lifelike sculptures of people, animals, and everyday objects, which probably graced the palaces of the nobility. Some of these are quite charming, such as a gentle-looking man holding a cacao pod, a feathered coyote, a smiling dog, a grasshopper carved in red stone, a conch shell, and a squash smoothly carved from green stone.

Precious Metal Workers

The metals most highly valued by the Aztecs were gold, silver, and copper. Copper was used for tools (axes, knives, needles, and fish hooks) and for adornment on costumes. The Aztecs knew how to mix copper and tin to produce bronze, but they never used bronze to any great extent. Although silver was important in the creation of jewelry and orna-mentation, gold was by far the most coveted metal.

Gold was obtained in regions bordering the Pacific Ocean by mining and panning. It was worked into jewelry and other types of ornamentation a variety of methods. One method was cold hammering, a technique in which metal is shaped without heating it first. Another method used by Aztec goldsmiths was the lost wax process. In this method, a model of the desired object is sculpted in wax and encased in a clay mold on which it leaves its impression. When the clay mold is fired, the wax melts off, leaving a perfect impression of the model on the inside of the mold. Molten gold is then poured into the space vacated by the wax and allowed to harden. When it cools, the mold is broken open and the finished article is removed.

While the Aztec nobility was fond of gold ornamentation, the conquering Spaniards were much more interested in gold for its market value. Consequently, only a few pieces of Aztec gold work escaped being melted into ingots for the Spanish treasury. The few pieces that remain are testimonies to the skill of Aztec goldsmiths.

One object discovered by archaeologists is a gold lip plug, an ornament that was placed in a hole made in a man's lower lip. It was cast in the shape of a serpent head and has a movable tongue. Another surviving example is a necklace of turquoise beads interspersed with tiny gold skulls. The lower jaw of each skull was cast as a separate piece. It was then loosely attached to the upper part of the skull so that the jaw moves up and down. Father Toribio Motolinia, a Spanish priest in Mexico, writes admiringly of the Aztec goldsmiths' skills. He says:

> They could cast a bird with a moveable tongue, head and wings, and cast a monkey

To fulfill certain quotas of the Aztec tribute system, women artisans of the common classes created high fashions for the privileged ladies of the nobility. In the following excerpt from his book *The History of the Indies of New Spain*, Spanish priest Diego Duran describes the fashions that the weavers and embroiderers created for wealthy Aztec women.

"Women's clothing was tributed: *huipiles* or loose blouses, also skirts, as well finished and splendid as it was possible to make, all of them enriched with wide borders embroidered in different colors and designs, with featherwork on the front; insignia done in colored thread: and on the back some of them bore embroidered flowers; others, imperial eagles. Still others were covered with flowers that were not only embroidered but were combined with featherwork, and these were a splendid thing to see. Beautiful skirts of great price were richly woven, with excellent skill. All of these clothes were used by the ladies who were wives and concubines of the lords and great chieftains. Another type of female dress arrived through tribute. This was entirely white and was worn by the young women and the old women who served in the temples."

or monsters with moveable head, tongue, feet, and hands, and in the hand put a toy so that it appeared to dance with it; and even more, they cast a piece, one half gold and one half silver, and cast a fish with all its scales, one scale of silver, one of gold, at which the Spanish goldsmiths would much marvel.[37]

Although feathers and gold were high on the list of luxury items desired by wealthy Aztecs, the list did not end there. Gemstones, mosaics, fine pottery, and exquisite fabrics were also prized, and the artisans who made them were handsomely rewarded.

Lapidaries

Aztec lapidaries created jewelry and other kinds of ornamentation from a variety of precious and semiprecious stones. "The favourite gemstones were jade, turquoise, and rock crystal," writes archaeologist Warwick Bray, "but Mexican lapidaries also worked in obsidian, amethyst, amber, bloodstone, carnelian, and a wide variety of coloured materials."[38]

Lapidary work entailed cutting, polishing, engraving, and mounting the stones, or sometimes creating objects from a single piece of stone. For example, exquisite bowls and ceremonial masks carved from single pieces of jade and obsidian have been recovered from archaeological sites. Another kind of lapidary work was the creation of mosaics from multicolored bits of turquoise and other colored stones. Mosaic work was used to cover many different kinds of objects, such as jewelry, pottery, shields, masks, and even human skulls.

Potters

The quality of Aztec pottery ran the gamut from cheaply made pieces to fine ceramics. Much of the everyday ware was made by pressing clay into molds, then joining the pieces together before firing. Many everyday items were made in this fashion, including plates, bowls, cups, pitchers, cooking vessels, incense burners, braziers, and griddles.

Highly skilled potters also made fine ceramics for wealthy patrons and for the temples. During the Templo Mayor excavation in Mexico City, two life-size figures of warriors made from molded terra-cotta clay were found in the temple ruins. Archaeologists also recovered many exquisitely made pottery vessels for use in the temples. Many of these artifacts are currently displayed at a museum on the site of the excavation.

The pottery most prized by the Aztecs, however, was not really Aztec at all. It came from Cholula, a region southeast of Tenochtitlán. The people of Cholula, who were living in the Valley of Mexico when the Aztecs arrived, had learned pottery designs and skills from their own ancestors. Cholula ware was thin, delicate, and beautifully decorated in colors of red, black, brown, yellow, and white. Díaz del Castillo comments in his memoirs that Montezuma's food was served to him on Cholula ware.

Weavers

Among the Aztecs, weaving fabrics was a woman's occupation that crossed all class lines. Even princesses learned to weave, but not everyone became an expert. Long strips

Aztec pottery included both cheaply made everyday ware to fine artistic pieces created by trained potters. The bowls in this picture were probably made and used in an Aztec household.

of cloth about a yard wide were woven on simple devices called belt looms. One end of the loom was attached to a tree or some other solid object. A belt or strap was attached to the other end so that it wrapped around the weaver's waist. This made it possible for her to control the tension on the loom by moving backward or forward.

Cloth was woven from cotton or maguey cactus fibers. Commoners were forbidden to wear cotton garments, but most of them could not have afforded them, anyway. Cotton had to be imported from the coastal regions of the empire and was therefore costly. Commoners' clothing was made from maguey fibers, which produced a stiffer fabric with a linenlike texture. Spinning the thread from either cotton or maguey plants was a complex job involving many steps. If colored fabrics were desired, the thread was dyed before it was woven with dyes made from plants. Another popular red dye called cochineal was made from the dried bodies of insects.

Weavers who became artisans at their trade were able to create borders, stripes, and intricate patterns in their designs. Another decoration technique was to stamp designs on fabrics with ceramic stamps into which a design had been carved. Rich and colorful embroidery was another technique. In a letter to King Charles V of Spain, Hernán Cortés describes gifts made of cotton that were given to him by Montezuma: "Montezuma gave me many garments of his own, which even considering that they were all of cotton and not silk were such that in all the world there could be none like them, nor any of such varied colors or such workmanship. Amongst them were very marvelous clothes for men and women, and there were bedspreads which could not have been compared even with silk ones."[39]

Basket and Mat Makers

Other crafters wove baskets, bags, mats, and seats from plant materials such as reeds, cane, palm leaves, and cacti of various kinds. All of these items were important for daily use in Aztec households that were otherwise sparsely furnished. Baskets were made in a great variety of sizes and shapes. Among them were strong, coarsely woven baskets for grain storage, rectangular baskets with lids for storing clothing and bedding in the home, and small, finely woven containers to hold jewelry and other special items.

"Closely related to the basket makers were the weavers of reed mats . . . and the makers of reed seats," writes historian Richard F. Townsend. "In ancient Mexico, furniture was limited to stools, litters, and low small tables. Mats . . . were an essential item in both royal and humble households where activities took place on or near the floor."[40]

A Gathering of Artisans

In the late 1980s, archaeologists working at a site near the Mexican city of Otumba were surprised to find that the people who had occupied the site had produced several different kinds of crafts. According to archaeologist Michael Smith, the archaeologists at the Otumba site "documented extensive craft production activity, including the manufacture of obsidian tools, pottery figurines and incense burners, textiles, and several types of jewelry."[41] Archaeologists had long known that Aztec families augmented their incomes by producing goods for the market, but the presence of so many craft producers at one place was surprising. "This unexpectedly high degree of craft specialization," Smith contin-

Templo Mayor Archaeological Project

An archaeological excavation in the center of Mexico City, called the Templo Mayor Project, began in 1978. Its purpose was to excavate the remains of the great Aztec temple that once stood in Tenochtitlán, the capital city of the Aztecs. In the process, many remarkable works were discovered, which are now displayed in a museum at the site. These excerpts are taken from Museo de Templo Mayor, the website produced by the Museum of the Templo Mayor, National Institute of Anthropology and History, Mexico (http://archaeology.la.asu.edu).

"Templo Mayor Project: The Templo Mayor Project arose from the accidental discovery of the Coyolxauhqui monolith [an eight-ton stone disk depicting an Aztec goddess] in 1978. This discovery led to a presidential decree authorizing a major exploration project, which was headed by Eduardo Matos Moctezuma who has continued to be in charge of the Project as well as director of the Museum. The Project's central objective is to rescue the remains of the Templo Mayor and associated objects and buildings, to preserve them, research them, and make information on all this work available to the public. After 20 years of uninterrupted labors, archaeological work and research have resulted in considerable new information on the Mexicas.

Templo Mayor Museum: Inaugurated on October 12, 1987, this site museum preserves, exhibits and publicizes information on archaeological materials excavated over the course of several seasons of work conducted by the Templo Mayor Project, from 1978 to the present. The museum has eight halls exhibiting thousands of objects . . . as well as sculptures, reliefs and other elements found in this area."

ues, "has changed our views of Aztec urbanism and economics."[42]

Discoveries such as this in the outlying areas raise new questions about the Aztec economic system. The basis of Aztec economy was indisputably agriculture, but industry and trade may have played greater roles than previously suspected.

5 Economy

As a whole, the economy of the Aztec Empire was based on farming, but it was augmented by industrial development (salt extraction, stone quarrying, and metallurgy), technological innovations (irrigation and dike systems), scientific inquiry (astronomy and botany), and a market and trading system for the distribution of goods and services. Thus, people in many different kinds of occupations helped make the empire stable, but the greatest burden, the production of corn and other food products, rested mainly on the shoulders of Aztec peasant farmers. In his book *Everyday Life of the Aztecs*, archaeologist Warwick Bray writes of the importance of this group:

> There is a natural tendency, shared by the Spanish chroniclers and modern archaeologists alike, to concentrate attention on the spectacular aspects of Mexican civilization and to forget that the cultured life of the towns would have been impossible without the taxes and tribute labour of the peasantry. . . . It was the food surplus produced by the countryside and the provinces which maintained the temples and armies, paid the salaries of the officials, and allowed the nobility to enjoy the comforts of city life.[43]

This fact was brought home to the Aztecs tragically when four successive years of drought, beginning in 1450, resulted in a terrible famine. Even though the rulers opened the reserve granaries and purchased food from other regions, thousands of Aztecs died of starvation. When the rains came again, bountiful harvests from several types of farming gradually restored the badly damaged economy.

Traditional Farming

Most farming was done in fields close to farmers' houses, using methods passed down for generations. The main farming tool was a *coa*, a long digging stick that fanned out at the bottom to form a kind of spade. Planting was done by digging holes with the *coa* and depositing seeds by hand. The Aztec cultivated many different kinds of edible plants. The major ones were several varieties of corn, beans, and squash. A traditional Aztec garden plot might also contain tomatoes, onions, chili peppers, amaranth (a grain), peanuts, sweet potatoes, pumpkins, prickly pear cactus, and various kinds of fruits. A special drink similar to hot chocolate was prepared from cacao beans that grew on trees in the tropical regions. Cacao beans were so highly prized that they were sometimes used as currency, and only the nobility was allowed to drink the beverage made from them.

Although peasant farmers were free citizens, they did not own the land they farmed. Farmland was controlled by the *calpulli* (residential clans) and was allotted to individual families by *calpulli* officials. Some members of the nobility owned large estates in the country granted to them by the emperor. Estate lands were worked by peasants called *mayeques*. Technically, *mayeques* were also free citizens, but like the serfs in medieval Europe, they were forbidden to leave the estates on which they worked.

Intensive Farming Systems

As the Aztec population grew larger and more urbanized, a great many people began working at occupations other than farming. To grow enough food both for themselves and the nonfarming population, Aztec farmers gradually improved their agricultural methods. They also began planting crops on terraced hillsides that had never before been cultivated.

In the late 1980s, archaeologist Michael E. Smith and his research team did field surveys and excavations at a hilly rural site in the Mexican state of Morelos. There they found remnants of terraced fields edged with rocks. They also discovered the ruins of many check dams that had been built to trap rainwater inside the terraced gardens. Excavations showed that, because silt eventually reached the top of the check dams, additional rows of rocks had been added many times.

Chinampa Farming

Another kind of intensive cultivation practiced by the Aztecs was *chinampa* farming. According to their own legends, the Aztecs began as a nomadic people who later settled on a small island in Lake Texcoco. Because

An Aztec farmer uses his hands to harvest amaranth, a grain the Aztecs widely cultivated.

there was so little room on the island for raising crops, Aztec farmers began building *chinampas* to create more land. *Chinampas* were long, rectangular structures made of stakes and branches that were attached to the bottom of the shallow lake. These marked-off areas were then filled with sludge dredged up from the lake bottom.

Once a *chinampa* was established, soil was added until it was slightly higher than the lake surface. Farmers then planted willow trees and other vegetation on the edges to anchor the little island in place. Rows of *chinampas* were built side by side with narrow channels left between them to allow for the passage of canoes.

Chinampas were very productive, supplying many tons of fruits and vegetables for the urban areas to which they were attached. Since there were no large farm animals in Mexico at that time to produce fertilizer, *chinampas* were fertilized with human waste. This arrangement also provided a way to deal with sewage problems that the urban areas faced. Removing sewage to the *chinampas* by canoe was another occupation engaged in by some Aztec commoners.

Chinampa Gardens

Whether the Aztecs originated the practice of *chinampa* farming is unknown, but they unquestionably made the most of this agricultural innovation. Historian David Carrasco explains why and how the Aztecs used this form of gardening in this excerpt from his book, *Daily Life of the Aztecs: People of the Sun and Earth.*

"One of the most productive agricultural achievements in pre-contact New World history was the *chinampa* system, consisting of long, rectangular gardens made from reclaimed swampland within or connected to the lakes of the Basin of Mexico. The peoples who migrated into Central Mexico in the thirteenth century were expert farmers and learned that the success of the *chinampa* system depended in part on the remarkably fertile soils in and around the lakes. During their early years around Lake Texcoco, the Aztecs developed their farming and military skills as they sought to attach themselves to the stronger city-states. They were eventually rejected by one of the most powerful communities and were driven off the mainland and forced to live on swamps. They responded by raising *chinampa* fields, which meant piling up vertical rows of mud and vegetation between pylons. . . . Thus each *chinampa* was a slender, rectangular strip of garden land 10 to 25 feet wide by 50 to 300 feet long. Farming families lived on these earthen platforms in houses made of cane, wood, and reeds. . . . Eventually, this system of gardening required a sophisticated bureaucracy to manage the irrigation, planting, and harvesting of corn, amaranth, squash and beans. It produced huge amounts of foodstuffs and flowers that contributed significantly to the rise and wealth of the city. . . . This system of farming was so productive that parts of the surfaces of three of the lakes (Chalco, Xochimilco, and Texcoco) were reduced from open lakes into networks of *chinampas* and canals. This also meant that the produce could be easily loaded from the *chinampas* into canoes and taken directly to the urban markets along the lakes and to markets in Tenochtitlan and Tlateloco."

Aztec workers build a chinampa, *a small, fenced-in plot of soil and sludge that was erected on stilts in shallow water.*

Other Food Industries

Workers in many occupations besides farming also supplied foods for the markets. These foods included fish and other aquatic delicacies, wild game, domesticated animals and fowls, and eggs of all kinds. After a trip to one of the great markets, Spanish soldier Bernal Díaz del Castillo wrote, "They were selling fowls, and birds with great dewlaps [turkeys], also rabbits, hares, deer, young ducks, little dogs, and other such creatures."[44] The dogs mentioned by Díaz del Castillo were a special breed raised specifically for the market and considered very tasty, even by the Spaniards.

Salt extraction was another important industry. The southern arm of Lake Texcoco contained freshwater, but the remainder of the lake was salty. During the dry season, salt workers scooped up earth containing salt granules from the dry lakebeds. The granules were separated out by washing, and the residue was boiled in huge pottery basins to evaporate the remaining moisture. The finished product was formed into loaves or cakes and sold in the markets.

Stone and Metal Industries

Other important industries not associated with food were mining and quarrying. While a great deal is known about the work of artisans who created artistic objects from metal and stone, less is known about those who produced the raw materials. These are the people who, in the words of historian David Carrasco, "held up the social pyramid on their hands, backs, skills, and abilities."[45]

Gold was not found in the Valley of Mexico, so the Aztec subjugated regions where gold was plentiful and demanded gold as tribute. Panning for gold in streams and rivers was the technique most widely used to get it. Some mining for gold and silver also took place. Mines were dug into the hillsides, where chunks of ore were extracted with chisels and stone hammers. The rock-bearing ore deposits were then crushed to free the metals.

Stone for temples, palaces, monuments, and statuary was plentiful in the mountainous terrain around the Valley of Mexico. The business of quarrying stone and transporting it was established well before the Aztec Empire began, and the techniques were passed down through time. Enormous stones weighing many tons were moved from quarries to building sites by rolling them on logs or simply by attaching ropes and dragging them into place.

Carrasco says of the stone cutters, "They were responsible for quarrying the stones, breaking them into large and small pieces, splitting them, curving them, and cutting them with great dexterity, turning them into everything from walkways to houses to monuments."[46] Wood workers and carpenters were important in the construction industry, also, but most of their work has not endured.

Other kinds of stone, such as obsidian, a black volcanic rock that looks like glass, were also mined. Archaeologists at Aztec sites find thousands of obsidian artifacts. Obsidian is a beautiful stone, often used for ornamentation, but its major attraction for the Aztecs was its sharpness in tools and weapons. Thin strips of obsidian were flaked from a block of stone by a technique called pressure flaking, a task that required great strength and precision. Flakes from the core were fitted into handles to make knives and sickles.

The razor sharpness of obsidian also made it a natural for weapons. Obsidian flakes were shaped into points for arrows and darts, and unworked pieces were inserted into the sides of wooden forms to make swords and spears. Aztec priests used razor-sharp daggers made of obsidian or flint to cut open the chests of sacrificial victims. The handles of the sacrificial daggers were often richly decorated with mosaics and carvings.

Aztec workers engaged in many other occupations as well. A list compiled from historic documents identifies thirty-four major types of businesses that flourished during the late Aztec period. Many of these businesses made use of scientific information from astronomy and botany.

Astronomy and the Solar Calendar

Like many Mesoamerican cultures before them, the Aztecs were ever mindful of the heavens as they watched for signs and omens from the gods. They tracked the movements of celestial bodies, identified many of the same constellations that are known today, and were even able to predict eclipses. Based on their observations, Aztec scholars developed a solar calendar that guided farming and fixed the dates of religious ceremonies and festivals. The solar calendar (sometimes called the round calendar) consisted of 360 days with five days added at the end of the cycle. These days were called "idle" or "hollow" days and believed to be very unlucky. "They did no work in those days," writes the Spanish priest Bernardino de Sahagún, "because they were considered unlucky, and they especially refrained from quarreling, because they said that anyone who quarreled in those days acquired the habit."[47] An extra day, similar to our leap year, was also added at intervals to synchronize the calendar with the solar year.

The Day Count

Another calendar that more closely affected the everyday lives of the Aztecs was the day count. Each day in this twenty-day calendar had its own symbol. *Crocodile* was the first symbol, followed in order by *wind, house, lizard, serpent, death, deer, rabbit, water, dog, monkey, grass, reed, jaguar, eagle, vulture, movement, flint, rain*, and *flower*.

The first thirteen days of the calendar were numbered consecutively from *1 crocodile* to *13 reed*. Then the count started all over again. The next symbol after *reed* was the jaguar, so that day became *1 jaguar* and ended with *13 death*. The symbol after the death sign was a deer, so the next sequence began with *1 deer* and so on in that manner. It took 260 days (13 days x 20 symbols) for the two counts to make a complete circle, that is, to come back to *1 crocodile*.

The result was that each of the 260 days of the cycle had a different designation. It was important to keep track of the days this way be-cause each day had its own significance. Art historian Elizabeth Hill Boone comments, "Each of the day signs and each of the day numbers carried meaning for the Aztecs; the gods, colors, directions, and rituals associated with each of these signs and numbers indicated what kind of day it would be. When the Aztec named the days, this was the count they used."[48]

Botany for Ornamentation and Healing

Another kind of scientific inquiry was botany, the study of plants. The Aztecs benefited greatly from botanical knowledge passed down by Mesoamerican cultures before them, but they also contributed discoveries of their own. In his history of the Aztecs, Sahagún mentions two types of agricultural workers, farmers and horticulturists. Farmers were the people who did the actual jobs of planting, irrigating, tending, and harvesting the various crops. Horticulturists were plant specialists who knew about soils, crop rotation, trees, herbs, medicinal plants, flowers, and seeds. They were often managers of agriculture projects such as the experimental botanical gardens established by several of the emperors.

Montezuma I (great-grandfather of Montezuma II, who ruled at the time of Cortés) had a botanical garden built at Huaxtepec, a sacred place near Tenochtitlán. Curious to see whether exotic plants from other regions could be grown there, he sent messengers to regions where such plants grew and asked for specimens. "The treasured plants were duly dug up with their roots encircled in earth," Townsend reports, "and then wrapped in textiles and transported to Huaxtepec. . . . Success was apparent before three years had passed, for the transplants began to blossom luxuriantly."[49]

Aztec scholars developed an elaborate solar calendar, a representation of which is seen here, to establish sowing and harvesting times, and to fix the dates of religious festivals.

An Aztec Herbal

In addition to their aesthetic value, plants were also valued by the Aztecs for healing. Herbalists studied the medicinal properties of plants and sold preparations made from them in the markets. Martinus de la Cruz, an Aztec physician, wrote the oldest known book about herbal medicines from the New World in 1552. The text was later translated from Nahuatl into Latin by Juannes Badianus. Both men had converted to Christianity after the conquest and were associated with the College of Santa Cruz in Mexico City.

Each page of the book, *An Aztec Herbal*, has a picture of a medicinal plant painted in vivid colors. A description of each plant and its medical uses is written below in Latin. The book is arranged into chapters according to body parts—remedies for the eyes, ears, abdomen, and so forth—or by various bodily afflictions. For instance, a cough may be relieved by drinking juice from the peeled and ground root of a cornsilk flower mixed with water and honey. The patient is also directed to smear the throat with the mixture and to chew some of the root dipped in honey. This root of this plant was also used in preparations to relieve diarrhea, dysentery, and indigestion. Another interesting entry in *An Aztec Herbal* is a remedy for "black blood," an old term for melancholia or mental depression:

> Both the ground leaves and roots of the herbs quauhtla huitzquilitl ["wild spiney edible plant"] and tlatlanquaye ["jointed stem"—a kind of pepper] are to be cooked in water; to which are to be added a pearl, a wolf's liver and our wine. He is to take the juice thus prepared as a drink. Before the mid-day meal he shall drink another juice pressed from good-smelling flowers of different kinds. He shall walk in a shady place, refrain from venery [sexual relations], drink our wine moderately, in fact, he should not drink it except as medicine. He shall engage in the very cheerful pursuits, such as singing or playing music and beating the tympans which we use in public dancing.[50]

Other Sciences

The fact that the Aztecs were technologically adept at engineering and mathematics is obvious from the ruins they left behind. Temples and other monumental buildings were constructed with precision and aligned with the path of the sun and other celestial bodies. Engineering expertise may also be seen in Aztec public works, such as the aqueducts that brought freshwater to the island city of Tenochtitlán and the dikes and locks that kept the salt water of Lake Texcoco from flowing into the freshwater arm. Scientific knowledge involving chemistry is apparent in the creation of pottery, alloys, concrete, and paints and fabric dyes whose vivid colors have lasted for centuries.

Aztec Markets, Trade, and Transportation

An essential part of any economic system is distribution—getting the food and other goods to markets where they are available to consumers. For a society with no draft animals or wheeled vehicles, the Aztec markets and trading networks were remarkable. They reached into the farthest corners of the empire and even beyond.

Although almost every village had a local market, the markets in the larger towns and cities were the ones that most astounded the

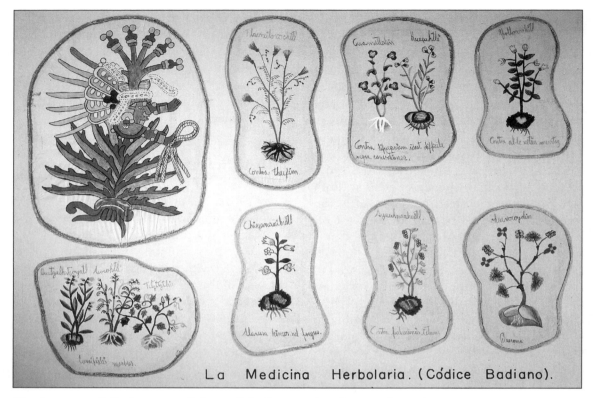

La   Medicina   Herbolaria.   (Códice   Badiano).

The Aztecs carefully documented the medicinal properties of many plants. A page from the Spanish book, The Aztec Herbal, *shows some of the plants they studied and used.*

Spaniards, particularly the great marketplace on the outskirts of Tenochtitlán. Reflecting upon his first visit there, Díaz del Castillo writes,

> On reaching the market-place, escorted by the many *Caciques* [chieftains] whom Montezuma had assigned to us, we were astounded at the great number of people and the quantities of merchandise, and at the orderliness and good arrangements that prevailed, for we had never seen such a thing before. The chieftains who accompanied us pointed everything out. Every kind of merchandise was kept separate and had its fixed place marked for it.[51]

The flow of trade goods that moved continuously throughout the empire was carried on the backs of hired porters. A load was placed on a wooden frame to which a band of leather or fabric was attached. The band, called a tumpline, fitted across the porter's forehead to support the load. Porters supposedly could carry a load of fifty pounds for fifteen miles, but that depended upon what they were carrying, the kind of terrain underfoot, and even the weather.

Porters also carried high-status people on two- or four-person platforms called litters. Long poles were attached underneath the litter on both sides. The poles were longer than the litter so that the protruding ends could be placed on the shoulders of the porters.

Obviously, the work of porters was hard, and although it was not a shameful occupation, porters were men of low status. The work was also physically damaging. Some sources say that the constant pressure on the porters' foreheads from the tumplines brought blood and left scars. It was also believed to cause baldness.

The services provided by porters, however, were essential to the economy. In order to keep a steady flow of goods moving over the roads and trails, their work was organized into districts and scheduled by local officials. This was especially important for tribute goods that had to be sent to Tenochtitlán periodically throughout the year.

Transport by canoes was much more efficient in places where they could be used. In a book about Aztec trading, anthropologist Ross Hassig writes, "The canoes in the valley of Mexico were dugouts—shallow draft, square bow craft hewn from single trees—and were of many varieties. They were rowed or poled, but lacked sails."[52] Canoes were vital to the economy of the lake area around Tenochtitlán, and many commoners were employed as canoe builders, dockworkers, rowers, and polers.

Although canoes were used to transport people, their major purpose was hauling food and other commodities to and from urban areas around the lakes. The speed at which a canoe traveled was no faster than a porter could walk carrying a load on his back, but a porter

Urban Markets

Except for the temple and palaces, the thing that impressed Spanish conquistador Hernán Cortés most about the Aztec city of Tenochtitlán was the enormous market area. Cortés's description of the market, written to Charles V, king of Spain, is taken from *Letters from Mexico*, by Hernán Cortés, translated and edited by A.R. Pagden.

"The city has many squares where trading is done and markets are held continuously. There is also one square twice as big as that of Salamanca [a city in Spain] with arcades all around, where more than sixty thousand people come each day to buy and sell, and where every kind of merchandise produced in these lands is found; provisions as well as ornaments of gold and silver, lead, brass, copper, tin, stones, shells, bones, and feathers. They also sell lime, hewn and unhewn stone, adobe bricks, tiles, and cut and uncut woods of various kinds. . . . They sell rabbits and hares and small gelded dogs which they breed for eating. There are streets of herbalists where all the medicinal herbs and roots found in the land are sold. . . . There are shops like barbers' where they have their hair washed and shaved, and shops where they sell food and drink. There are also men like porters to carry loads.

Each kind of merchandise is sold in its own street without any mixture whatever; they are very particular in this. . . . There is in this great square a very large building like a courthouse, where ten or twelve persons sit as judges. They preside over all that happens in the markets, and sentence criminals. There are in this square other persons who walk among the people to see what they are selling and the measures they are using; and they have been seen to break some that were false."

could carry only a fraction of the weight carried by canoe. The length of the canoes varied from fourteen to fifty feet, with the largest canoes capable of carrying sixty passengers or about four tons of weight. The number of canoes in use at the height of the empire may have been more than one hundred thousand.

Merchants

Aztec merchants were of two basic types—local and long-distance. Local merchants were peddlers and marketplace vendors in their own areas, while long-distance traders, called *pochtecas*, traveled in caravans to distant regions for weeks at a time. Their work was dangerous and exhausting. The terrain over which they traveled was rugged, and everything had to be carried on the backs of human porters. Long-distance trade was risky in other ways as well. Bandits sometimes preyed upon caravans, and merchants often had to travel across territories that were hostile to the Aztecs.

The rewards of long-distance trading were great, however. The *pochtecas* were at the top of the common social class system. They lived in their own neighborhoods, worshipped their own gods, and even had their own court sys-

Aztec cities had busy marketplaces where both basic provisions and exotic wares were for sale.

Merchant Spies

Long-distance merchants (*pochtecas*) in the Aztec Empire sometimes acted as spies for the government as they went about their trading business. In this excerpt from *Aztec Warfare*, author Ross Hassig explains why merchants made good undercover agents and tells of the dangers they faced when gathering intelligence.

"General information could be gleaned from many sources, including returning troops and travelers, but perhaps the most useful and organized conduits of general intelligence were the merchants. . . . Not only did they travel throughout the Aztec Empire, they also went beyond it to trade with independent groups owing no allegiance to Tenochtitlan. . . . Much of the merchants' intelligence gathering was incidental to their primary trading functions, but they were sometimes given intelligence duties to perform for the state. . . .

On at least some occasions when entering hostile areas beyond the Aztec Empire, the merchants disguised themselves as natives of other areas, cutting their hair in the local manner and learning the language, because if they had been discovered, they would have been killed.

Killing a merchant was a just cause of war in Mesoamerica, and such incidents initiated many wars. . . . On other occasions the merchants passed through enemy lands armed with shields and swords, as if prepared for war. They met with some success when battle was thrust upon them and were rewarded by the king in the same manner as valiant warriors. If the merchants were openly attacked or were besieged, the king sent warriors to their aid. Although flight was not honored among warriors, it was rewarded among merchants because of the emphasis of obtaining their information."

tem. They formed powerful trade guilds to protect their interests, and as a result, most of them were very rich. In spite of their privileged status, however, the *pochtecas* operated their trading businesses quietly and were forbidden to show off their wealth.

Another reason for being secretive about long-distance trading was that *pochtecas* frequently acted as spies for the emperor. They spied on the defenses in unconquered territories and on city-state rulers who might be withholding tribute or planning an uprising. Merchant spies were heavily armed and ready to do battle if necessary. In the Aztec Empire, it often was necessary, because the conduct of war was basic to the existence of the empire.

6 Warfare

War was a fact of life in Aztec society. The empire was built and maintained on warfare or the threat of it. During lulls when there was no major fighting, the Triple Alliance conducted "flowery" wars against a common enemy just to train new warriors, keep veterans in top fighting form, and maintain a steady flow of prisoners for sacrifice.

The purpose of war for the Aztecs was to gain tribute from conquered peoples rather than to colonize or govern their territories. The type of warfare the Aztecs conducted was geared to that end—to force a surrender of an enemy by combat or negotiation, to draw up a contract of tribute expected from the vanquished, and to severely punish those groups who failed to live up to the demands or who showed signs of rebellion. The punishment served as a deterrent to other groups who might be tempted to rebel.

Because war was also a religious matter, it provided a means of capturing sacrificial victims called for in Aztec religious observances. Moreover, capturing prisoners gave Aztec warriors an incentive to fight because great honors were heaped on those who brought captives back after a battle. In order to gain all of these objectives, the Aztec war machine was highly organized, disciplined, and effective.

Organization of the Army

Although the Aztecs had professional warriors, most of the troops consisted of commoners who had to make a living in other ways. Therefore, no large-scale standing army existed. When the need arose, as it often did, a call to arms was issued and men were conscripted from different areas depending upon where the action was taking place and whose turn it was on a rotating schedule of service.

In his book *Aztec Warfare*, anthropologist Ross Hassig points out that there are no surviving documents that explain the ranking system and overall organization of the Aztec army. From bits of existing information, however, it appears that army organization closely followed the social class structure. The highest ranks were filled by elite members of the nobility, lesser ranks by lesser nobles, and so on down to the common foot soldiers at the bottom of the pyramid.

However, the system was not entirely closed to advancement for commoners. Hassig comments, "Historical accounts place the greatest emphasis on the elite warriors, but most of the army was composed of commoners without military distinction. It was possible to rise from this status by virtue of one's deeds and ability, but social class did influence one's military career, despite the emphasis on advancement by merit."[53]

Projectile Weapons

Important offensive weapons used by Aztec armies included those designed to launch a projectile of some type, such as arrows shot from bows, darts thrown with the use of a special device called an atlatl, and rocks flung from slings. Common soldiers were more apt to use projectile weapons in battle than elite soldiers. Many commoners had experience with bows, slings, and darts, which were also used in hunting. While almost anyone could use projectile weapons, there were those who excelled in the use of each type. For instance, Hassig reports, "The archers of Teohuacan were reputedly so skilled they could shoot two or three arrows at a time as skillfully as most could shoot one."[54] Aztec bows were about five feet long, with bowstrings made of animal sinew or hide. Arrows made of reeds were tipped with obsidian, which was equal to steel in its penetrating power.

Darts and dart throwers were also formidable projectile weapons. The dart thrower, or atlatl, was a wooden stick used to propel a dart with much more force than could be attained by simply throwing a spear. The points on the darts were made of obsidian, bone, flint, or copper, and some of them were barbed, or pronged, to make them hard to remove.

Aztec priests remove the heart from a live human sacrifice, most likely a prisoner of war, in this Spanish illustration.

By their own reports, it was the rocks thrown at them from slings made of maguey fiber that gave the Spaniards the most trouble in fighting the Aztecs. In a letter to the king of Spain, conquistador Hernán Cortés tells of a fierce battle that occurred when he and his Indian allies were trying to invade the city of Tenochtitlán. To get across the bridges leading to the city, Cortés's men built wooden structures (called engines) to protect their troops. Cortés writes:

> When we reached one of the bridges we placed the engines against the wall of a house and set up ladders with which to climb onto the roof, but there were so many people defending the bridge and the roof top, and so many and so large were the stones which they threw down at us, that they put our engines out of action and killed one Spaniard and wounded many more. We were unable to advance one step, although we fought hard from morning until midday, at which hour we returned to the fortress sorely disappointed.[55]

Shock Weapons

Shock weapons were offensive weapons designed to be held in the hands for close combat. Aztec shock troops used spears to thrust and slash the enemy. They also used clubs of various types and wooden swords whose cutting edges were made from flint or obsidian. Some swords were wielded with one hand. Larger ones required both hands, which left the warrior without protection from a shield.

Fighting with shock weapons required more training than fighting with projectile weapons. Consequently, shock weapons were used mostly by elite warriors for hand-to-

hand combat. Moreover, elite soldiers were much better equipped with protective clothing for this type of fighting than common soldiers, who had no armor. No doubt, personal ambition also had something to do with who did the hand-to-hand fighting, as close combat provided greater opportunities to take captives and win honors.

Some scholars add noise to the list of offensive weapons used by the Aztecs. At the onset of hostilities, the attacking army rushed forward with hideous shouts, noisemakers, whistles, drums, and eerie tones created by blowing on large conch shells. The purpose of the noise was to terrify enemies and break their concentration.

Battle Dress

An Aztec army in the field was a colorful sight, with warriors wearing many different types of battle dress. "The troops did not wear uniforms," archaeologist Warwick Bray observes. "Each soldier dressed as he saw fit, putting on all the trappings to which his rank and military record entitled him, so that a warrior's status was obvious at once from his costume, insignia, and even hairstyle."[56]

Protective measures included body armor, shields, and helmets. Elite warriors wore quilted body armor, which only they could afford. It was made of two pieces of cotton fabric with a layer of unspun cotton sewn between the layers. Several types of protective garments were made from it, such as vests and tunics to cover the upper body. Quilted armor was about two inches thick and could actually stop arrows. Some of the Spanish soldiers adopted it in place of the heavy metal breastplates they usually wore.

Commanders and other high-ranking warriors wore distinctive hairstyles and helmets

Aztec warriors wore headdresses decorated with feathers and other ornaments to indicate their rank.

Battle Dress for Nobles

In 1556, a collection of works about the Americas was published in Italy. The collection included a highly regarded manuscript about the Aztecs originally written in Spanish and translated into Italian. The author was identified only as "a gentleman [or companion] of Cortes," probably one of his officers. To this day, no one knows who wrote it, so bibliographic references attribute it to the Anonymous Conqueror. Below is an excerpt from the manuscript of the Anonymous Conqueror about the battle dress of noble Aztec warriors. The excerpt is taken from *Narrative of Some Things of New Spain and of the Great City of Temestitan* [Tenochtitlán] *Mexico Written by a Companion of Hernan Cortes, the Anonymous Conqueror*. It is edited by Alec Christensen and found on the website of the Foundation for the Advancement of Mesoamerican Studies (www.famsi.org).

"The armor which they use in war are certain loose garments like doublets made of quilted cotton, a finger and a half thick, and sometimes two fingers; they are very strong. Over them they wear a doublet and hose all one garment, which are corded behind. This garment is made of thick cloth and is covered with a layer of feathers of different colors, making a fine effect. Some companies of soldiers wear white and crimson, others blue and yellow, and others again of different styles. The Lords wear over everything garments like short jackets, which with us are of chain mail, but theirs are of gold and silver gilt. These feather garments are in proportion to their weapons, for neither arrows nor darts pierce them, but are thrown back without making any wound, and even with swords it is difficult to penetrate through them. To guard the head they carry things like the heads of serpents, tigers, lions, or wolves, with open jaws, and the head of the man is inside the head of the creature as if it was being devoured. They are of wood covered over with feathers and with jewels of gold and precious stones, which is a wonderful sight. They use shields of various kinds, made of good thick reeds which grow in that country, interwoven with cotton of double thickness, and they cover them with precious stones and round plates of gold, which makes them so strong that nothing can go through, unless from a good crossbow. Some arrows it is true pierced them, but could do them no harm."

decorated with feathers and other ornaments to indicate rank and valorous deeds. Officers wore richly decorated body suits, often made of feathers, over their cotton armor. Sometimes they wore wristlets, armbands, and shin guards that were protective yet not cumbersome enough to interfere with movement. Nobles also wore leather sandals with an enclosed heel, a protective piece over the instep, and straps and thongs to keep them in place.

To complete the battle dress, warriors carried round shields on their left arms. The shields were made of wood, tightly woven reeds, or other hard-surfaced materials. Shields belonging to nobles were beautifully decorated with feather work in geometric and animal designs or sometimes the personal insignia of the warrior. Feather work was not just for show. The tightly sewn feather designs with their stiff backings could actually deflect darts and arrows. Common foot soldiers were not so well protected. Most of them carried shields, but they had to make do without protective armor or even sandals for their feet.

Military Societies

Outstanding Aztec warriors, both commoners and nobles, were members of an elite military corps that acted as shock troops in battle. This corps consisted of several different societies, including the prestigious jaguar and eagle groups. Membership in the different societies was based upon the number of captives a warrior had taken in battle as well as other exceptional acts of bravery.

Each society had its own distinctive battle dress, which sometimes indicated social standing as well as courage. For instance, jaguar warriors from the common classes wore the skins and heads of real jaguars, while nobles' battle costumes were made of feathers to resemble jaguar skin. Warriors of the eagle society wore costumes and headdresses fashioned in the likeness of eagles. In the late 1980s, life-size figures of two eagle warriors were found at the Templo Mayor archaeological excavation in Mexico City. The dramatic figures were made from terra-cotta, a kind of clay. "The face of the individual inside the bird's head, with its enormous beak, is a brilliant example of Aztec aesthetics," writes archaeologist Eduardo Matos Moctezuma. "The total expression of these figures is not only an example of the extent of utilization of clay the Aztecs achieved, but it succeeds in reproducing the dignity and fierce quality of the warriors of Huitzilopochtli."[57]

The Call to Battle

An Aztec emperor might decide to go to war for several reasons—when long-distance traders were murdered during trading expeditions, when city-states refused to meet tribute demands, when open rebellion broke out, or when an independent society refused an invitation to "join" the Aztec Empire. In the first three cases, the response was swift and sure, with troops being mobilized and sent as soon as possible.

In the last instance, a region that was reluctant to become a part of the empire would receive a visit from an official delegation asking the rulers to reconsider. Twenty days later, the delegation returned to get an answer. A second refusal received a stern warning with a few more days to think about the offer. After a third refusal, or sometimes a fourth, Aztec troops were on their way.

The mobilization call went out to the towns and cities of the empire and to the other Triple Alliance partners by messengers. How many soldiers were mobilized depended upon the seriousness, magnitude, and location of the threat. Nobles and military society warriors who were not involved in farming and other occupations handled minor threats close to Tenochtitlán. Handling major problems farther from Tenochtitlán required extensive logistical planning involving the mobilization of thousands of men from all social classes. Getting troops and battle equipment to a distant site without vehicles or draft animals was a formidable task. Outside Tenochtitlán and other cities around Lake Texcoco, there were no surfaced roads. Towns in the outlying areas were connected only by narrow dirt lanes on which travelers walked single file or, sometimes, two abreast.

Nevertheless, Aztec strategic planners were equal to the task. For instance, the march to battle was timed and scheduled to prevent congestion along the way. Aztec priests were the first group to leave Tenochtitlán, carrying statues of the gods. The next day, the generals, nobles, and high-status warriors began to march. If the emperor decided to go, he went in this contingent with a large corps of bodyguards. On the following two

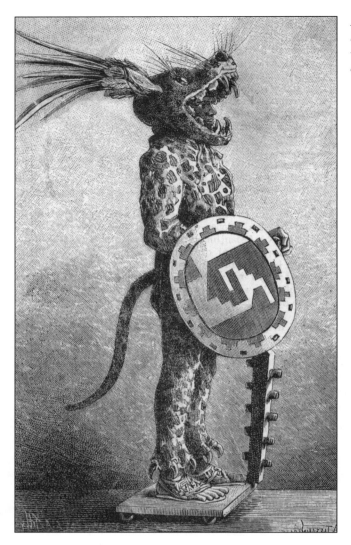

Aztec warriors like the one pictured to the left wore distinctive robes and wielded various weapons as a mark of their degree of bravery in battle.

days, more warriors from Tenochtitlán and those from other members of the Triple Alliance joined the march. Warriors from outlying towns joined in at the end and stayed together throughout the campaign. Scouts played a crucial role in the march to battle as well. Forward scouts provided intelligence about the enemy's defenses for the battle strategists. They also kept an eye out for possible attacks on the line of march, which stretched for miles.

Other major problems on the march were transporting baggage and feeding the troops. In the matter of transport, each soldier carried as much of his own personal belongings as possible. Beyond that, porters were hired (or provided their services as tribute) to move supplies and equipment for the campaign. Hassig estimates that on major campaigns the Aztecs had roughly one porter for every two warriors.

Some of the food for the troops was provided from army stores carried by the porters, but towns and cities on or near the march route were obliged to supply food for the troops as they came through. Settlements off the main route were expected to bring their contributions to the march route at their own expense. Food contributions were often required as tribute, but in addition, all towns were required by law to set aside a certain percentage of food and other goods each year just for military purposes. "The obligation to provide goods for the passing army was well understood, even if not always happily undertaken," Hassig comments. "Failure to meet these tributary obligations was considered an act of rebellion and could prompt the sacking of the town as could abandonment of the town in the face of the Aztec arrival."[58]

Making Camp

Aztec priests, the army commander (often the emperor himself), nobles, and high-status warriors of the military societies arrived first and set up a campsite near the city to be attacked. Although warriors sometimes used surprise attacks when the enemy was small in number and nearby, massive troop movements could not be kept secret. Usually, the people in the targeted cities were well aware

---

Flower Wars

During times when no major wars were being waged, the rulers of the Triple Alliance sometimes challenged the rulers of regions they had not been able to defeat to participate in "flower wars." These formalized skirmishes were taken seriously by the combatants, however, and warriors were killed and captives taken. In the excerpt below, taken from *The History of the Indies of New Spain*, author Diego Duran describes a flower war begun by the Aztecs that did not end well.

"[King Motecuhzoma] became weary of so much idleness and of the fact that there was no war in which his soldiers could practice their arts. Therefore, he decided to provoke the people of Huexotzinco. . . . With this decision made, Motecuhzoma immediately sent his messengers to challenge the cities. . . . The men of Huexotzinco, on hearing this challenge, accepted it with goodwill. They sent a message saying that they were well pleased and that three days later they would wait for the Aztecs in the valley.

One hundred thousand [Aztec] soldiers, the finest and most illustrious men of the three kingdoms, met upon the battlefield, all of them in splendid array. The Huexotzincas then appeared, no less finely attired and in equally good spirits, looking as if they had come to a festival. . . . Both sides went into the battle with such spirit that men began to fall on either side . . . a great slaughter took place, the men on both sides behaving like ferocious mountain lions drenched in blood. [When the Huexotzinca warriors refused to give up, Motecuhzoma's three brothers entered the battle and all three were killed.] Motecuhzoma was notified of the death of his brothers and his noblemen. He was also told how his army had been routed. When he heard this sad news, he began to weep bitterly for the loss of his brothers and the other warriors. The tidings spread throughout the city and everyone sobbed in sadness and despair. . . . The conch shells, trumpets, flutes, and drums, which usually sounded victory, on this day were mute."

that the Aztecs were coming and were busy preparing to defend themselves while the Aztecs were setting up camp.

If the emperor was present, a luxurious tent shelter was prepared for him immediately. Tents for nobles were set up nearby, for it was their job to protect the emperor in case of a surprise attack. Another large tent was pitched to protect the nobles' arms and other baggage. Makeshift fortifications were erected, and scouts were sent out to gather critical information for the coming battle. Guards and lookouts were posted around the clock.

Because of the staggered marching order, troops arrived in camp continuously for several days. Those who marched together also camped together, and each unit had its own leader. Food was distributed to each unit out of army stores, but the units were responsible for getting their own water and firewood. Warriors slept in tents or huts made of grass mats. When all the troops had arrived and plans were finalized, it was time to attack the enemy.

Engaging the Enemy

Aztec warriors were almost always greater in number than their opponents. For this reason, one of their main battle strategies was to encircle the enemy to cut off a retreat. Exactly how the Aztecs deployed their troops in battle is not clear. Nigel Davies, an anthropologist who has studied the Aztecs extensively, remarks, "We can name the different kinds of leaders, both generals and officers, and describe how they dressed, including the most precise details of their coiffure, but we are unable to say what were the exact duties of each."[59] Nevertheless, scholars have gleaned enough information from various sources to understand the basics of Aztec battle strategy.

Battles had strict rules and procedures. No one was to move against the enemy until a signal from the commander was given—a blast from a conch shell or the sound of a drum. When the signal came, warriors armed with bows, slings, and atlatls began firing a barrage of arrows, rocks, and darts as the battle line slowly advanced. The enemy forces stood their ground and replied with a projectile volley of their own.

This phase could continue only as long as the supply of projectiles lasted, however. Warriors could carry only a few arrows, darts, and rocks with them, and when these were depleted, hand-to-hand combat began. Veteran warriors of the prestigious military orders were in the forefront of the attack to act as shock troops. As they attacked, they set up a terrible racket of shouting and noise to distract and terrify their opponents. Although the object was to take captives, many of these encounters were bitterly fought and ended in death for one or both men.

Behind the shock troops came divisions of common soldiers under the command of their own leaders. In the confusion and noise of battle, it was important to know where the division leader was as well as to recognize members of one's own troop. To that end, division leaders attached tall bamboo frames to their backs with identifying logos or ornaments on them (which also made them prime targets for enemy warriors). Warriors painted their faces to distinguish themselves from the enemy and to identify themselves as members of their own division. Since most of the common soldiers lacked protective armor, the death rate among them was very high.

Battle Outcomes

A battle could end in various ways. Once it was obvious that the defenders' cause was lost, they

After besieging the city of Tenochtitlan for many months, Spanish conquerors fight their way back into the city in 1521, bringing an end to the Aztec Empire.

might negotiate a settlement to prevent having their city destroyed. That was the preferable conclusion for the Aztecs, since their goal was to receive tribute from the conquered city, not destroy it. If the defenders refused to give up, the Aztecs tried to capture and burn the temple inside the city. When that happened, surrender was almost assured. However, if the defenders still persisted in fighting, their city was looted, razed, and burned, and sometimes the entire population was slain.

Diego Duran, a Spanish missionary to Mexico, wrote a history of the Aztecs not long after the conquest. Taking his information from native informants, Duran describes a battle that was won by the Aztecs:

When the Aztecs saw that they were winning, they began to press on in such a way that the [enemy] soldiers from Tecuantepec and the other towns began to lose heart and flee from the field. They went up into the rugged places, fleeing from the Aztecs, who, with no pity at all, killed everyone they caught, without pardoning the life of any. [The Aztecs were fighting too far away from Tenochtitlán to take prisoners.] The lords of those cities, seeing this catastrophe and realizing that resistance to the Aztecs had ceased, begged for mercy, prostrating themselves on the ground before Ahuitzotl [the Aztec emperor] who, as furious as his men, was fighting alongside them. But he was moved by these entreaties and so sounded his drum, signaling retreat.[60]

The Aztec warriors, however, continued to loot after the retreat signal was given. When Emperor Ahuitzotl sent more troops in to stop the looting, the warriors complained that looting was their only compensation for risking their lives so far away from home. The king then promised to pay them with tribute gifts, and peace was restored. After that, negotiations were made for tribute from the lords of the conquered city, and the army moved on to the next battle.

Mourning the War Dead

In the following excerpt, Spanish missionary Father Diego Duran describes the funeral rites held for Aztec warriors killed in a battle against the city of Chalco during the reign of Emperor Montezuma I. The excerpt is taken from Father Duran's book, *The History of the Indies of New Spain*.

"When the Aztec soldiers reached Tenochtitlan, all the inhabitants went out to meet them with much rejoicing. The priests also were festive and appeared carrying braziers and incense burners. . . . After everyone had calmed down, was tranquil, and the army had rested from the toils of the recent war, the king ordered that honors and funeral rites be held for all those killed in the war. . . . Motecuhzoma ordered all the old songmakers whose occupation it was to mourn deaths such as these to compose songs that were appropriate for the occasion. So these old men composed chants for the dead, and when they were ready they came out with a drum that was hoarse and dissonant, and began to sing those mournful, sad dirges. Then the widows of the deceased, their sons and daughters, and all their relatives, came out after the chanters. All the women wore their hair loose, hanging close to their faces. They wore their husbands' mantles and breechcloths draped over one shoulder, while the sons and daughters carried in their hands their fathers' ear ornaments, feathers, and labrets [lip plugs], and all their fathers' jewels.

When all were in order, they began to dance and sing, with a strange wailing sound. . . . All the men who were kinsmen of the dead warriors—fathers, grandfathers, uncles, cousins, brothers—carrying the swords and shields of the deceased, formed a large circle. After they had danced quite a long time, they sat down to rest. [This was only the beginning of mourning rites that continued for eighty days.]"

On rare occasions when the Aztecs were losing a battle, the signal to retreat was heeded quickly. Warriors were trained to retreat in an orderly fashion to prevent loss of discipline. Troops moved backward in a certain order, still firing projectiles to hold off the enemy. In this situation, the veteran warriors were at the back of the troops to prevent encirclement.

Aftermath

The bodies of commoners who died in combat usually were cremated immediately, while the bodies of nobles were taken back to their families. Wounded soldiers were returned to the camp to be treated and cared for as well as possible. The unfortunate battle captives were made secure before marching back to Tenochtitlán and other Aztec cities, where they would be sacrificed to the Aztecs' gods.

Swift messengers were sent out to carry the outcome of the battle to the people in Tenochtitlán and other towns and cities. If the news was good, the troops received a rousing welcome as they made their way home. Bad news caused great mourning among the general population, and returning warriors on their homeward journey entered the towns weeping. Older warriors who acted as military advisers informed and consoled the families of those who had died in combat. Aztec warriors who were captured by the enemy were supposed to meet their fate as sacrificial victims to the gods of their captors with courage and dignity. Captured Aztec warriors who managed to escape and return home were looked upon with scorn and disgust.

In his book *The Aztec Empire*, anthropologist Nigel Davies discusses what made the Aztec army so successful. He asserts that it was not better weapons, smarter military leaders, or even superior warrior training, since all Mesoamerican societies were comparable in those matters. What set the Aztecs apart, Davies contends, was their carefully planned logistics and the gathering of intelligence before attacking an enemy. "The Aztecs performed extraordinary feats in deploying major forces over great distances," Davies writes. "This ability was reinforced by an excellent system of intelligence, to which the *pochtecas* [long-distance traders] made a great contribution."[61] Some scholars add another component—religious zeal. War to the Aztecs was a holy crusade and a sacred duty.

Religion

In Aztec society, religion was not a separate institution but was woven into every aspect of life from cradle to grave. Many of the Aztec gods and rituals had existed in Mesoamerican cultures for centuries, but many others were unique to the Aztecs. The Aztec religious system was tightly organized and closely linked to the state. However, considerable diversity existed as people in the city-states worshipped their own patron gods as well as the principal gods of the empire.

Intellectual Aztecs conceived of the supreme god as a single, invisible, all-powerful force that was both male and female. All other gods were only manifestations of this supreme deity. This concept was not widely shared among the people, however, who looked upon the numerous gods as real and personal.

Religious Organization

The Aztec religious institution was organized much like the governmental structure, with the emperor at the top. Although the emperor was not a priest, he was the earthly representation of the Aztec patron god and god of war, Huitzilopochtli. Next in descending order were two high priests who served at the Templo Mayor (main temple) in Tenochtitlán. One of the high priests served Huitzilopochti, whose shrine stood atop the Templo Mayor. The other was dedicated to Tlaloc, the god of rain, whose shrine stood next to that of the war god.

Below the high priests were a select group of men called fire priests. "These priests were responsible for the performance of the highest ritual—human sacrifice," archaeologist Michael E. Smith reports. "Regular priests assisted at the stone of sacrifice, but only a fire priest could wield the lethal flint knife."[62] Below the fire priests were many subordinate positions filled by priests of lesser status.

The priesthood was undoubtedly the best way to move up in a tightly closed social system. A boy or girl from any social class could be dedicated to the priesthood by the parents when the child was very young. Not all inductees remained with the priesthood, however. Women usually served for a time and then left to be married, and some men did the same. Of those who remained, the most promising were selected to become full priests and priestesses.

The duties of priests included performing sacred rites and rituals, maintaining the temples and estate lands, performing administrative duties, and educating children in the *calmecac* schools. Priests were also expected to make blood sacrifice regularly by cutting themselves or puncturing their skin with cactus spines. Chronicles written by eyewitnesses say that priests were extremely unpleasant to look at after years of this practice. Their bodies were scarred and their hair, which they never cut, washed, or combed, was matted with blood.

Priestesses taught in the schools and performed in festivals honoring goddesses and other deities associated with fertility and childbirth. Historian David Carrasco describes a scene from such a festival:

During the sacred ceremony of *Quecholli*, the young priestesses dedicated to the goddess of maize carried seven ears of corn wrapped in cloth throughout parts of the procession. They were transformed into images of the goddess and wore feathers on their arms and legs and had their faces painted with fertility colors. They sang and processed through the streets until sundown, when they tossed handfuls of colored maize kernels and pumpkin seeds in front of the crowds. The people scrambled to get these seeds because they were signs that the coming year would have a good harvest.[63]

The origin and meaning of religious practices such as these have roots in the worldview of a society. A society's worldview includes basic beliefs about how the world

This terra-cotta statue of an Aztec priest wearing the disk earrings and fierce look of the fire god reveals how intimately Aztec priests identified with their gods.

came to be, how people were created, the nature of the deities, ideas of good and evil, and attitudes toward life.

Aztec Worldview

Aztecs pictured the earth as a flat disk surrounded by water. Stretched above it were seven layers of heaven and below it nine layers of hell. It was within these layers that the gods lived, but they could also enter the earth in various forms and guises. The universal god, Ometeotl, had a dual nature, being both male and female. This duality was expressed in a god and goddess called the Lord and Lady of Our Sustenance. The four sons born to this couple were granted the power to create other gods, the world, and everything in it, including people. "Of the four gods," writes archaeologist Warwick Bray, "the two most important are Quetzalcoatl, a benevolent deity and friend of mankind, and Tezcatlipoca, an omnipotent being who was the god of darkness and sorcery. These two divinities were rivals, and during the course of their struggle for supremacy the universe was created and destroyed four times."[64]

After the fourth destruction, the gods all met at Teotihuacan, the ruins of a sacred city near Tenochtitlán, to make a plan for a fifth world. Since the sun was necessary to sustain life on earth, one of the gods sacrificed himself in a fire to become the sun. Although the transformation was successful, the new sun was unable to move across the sky by itself. When all other efforts to move the sun failed, many gods threw themselves into the fire and were reborn in the sky to help the sun make its daily journey. Thus the fifth world began.

The fifth world was the one in which the Aztecs lived, but at first there were no people in it. Undergoing much danger and suffering, Quetzalcoatl went to the lowest regions of hell to gather the bones of humans who had lived in previous worlds. From these bones and with his own blood, he re-created people. Obviously, the people owed a great debt to the gods for restoring the world and human life. One way to repay the debt was to send the souls of sacrificed warriors to the sky to assist the sun in its struggle against the forces of darkness. Without this daily assistance, the sun would die and the fifth world would end violently as the previous four worlds had done.

Sacrifice of Slaves and Captive Warriors

Although human sacrifice in religious rites was practiced in many other Mesoamerican cultures, it was most prevalent among the Aztecs. Not only were daily sacrifices to Huitzilopochtli made, but also hundreds of people were sacrificed regularly at festivals held in each of the eighteen months of the Aztec year. Sacrificial victims for the festivals were mostly slaves from conquered areas and captives taken in hand-to-hand combat.

Many enemy women, children, and non-fighting men were rounded up after a battle and taken back to cities and towns as slaves. However, methods used to capture warriors in the midst of a battle are not clearly understood. For instance, a captive warrior would have to be able to walk back with the conquering troops, raising the question of how an Aztec warrior could capture an enemy without seriously wounding him. If the enemy warrior had not been seriously wounded, why would he stop fighting, knowing full well what would happen to him if he surrendered?

Anthropologist Nigel Davies suggests that captives may have been rounded up by spe-

This illustration from a codex depicts a human sacrifice to the sun god. Sacrificial victims were mostly slaves from conquered areas and captive enemy warriors.

cial groups of warriors on the battlefield while the fighting was going on. "In addition," Davies suggests, "the sources often mention the use of the ambush by the Aztecs and by their opponents. These tactics were successful in one of Montezuma I's campaigns, for example; the Aztecs fell on their opponents from front and rear and took many prisoners.

Those enemies who were not killed were taken off to Tenochtitlán as captives."[65]

By whatever methods enemy warriors were obtained, they and captured slaves were sacrificed in great numbers each year, not only in Tenochtitlán, but in many other Aztec cities as well. As a rule, captives were well treated before being slain. They were given food, bathed, and dressed in fine cloaks. The captors reassured their victims that they were performing a sacred duty and that, upon death, their souls would fly to heaven to be with the sun god. This gentle treatment usually continued for several days before the doomed captives were led to places of sacrifice. One such location was at the top of the temple pyramid, where priests, matted and stained with the blood of other victims, awaited them. Some victims struggled, some fainted, and some were given drinks of intoxicating pulque to dull their minds. Most victims, however, calmly walked to their deaths.

When a victim reached the top of the pyramid, he was snatched by four men who threw him on his back across a sacrificial stone. With one slash from the priest's long obsidian knife, his chest was opened. The priest then literally tore out his heart, held it up to the sun, and then placed it in a special bowl. The victim's body was thrown down the steps of the pyramid, where it was dismembered and decapitated. The arms and legs were cooked and later eaten ceremoniously by the captor and his family. The skin was removed from the victim's skull, and the skull was mounted in a rack in front of the temple along with hundreds of others.

Account of the Women Who Served in the Temple

Girls of all social classes could be dedicated to the priesthood by their parents when they were still very young. In the following excerpt from *History of the Things of New Spain*, Spanish priest Bernardino de Sahagún describes the steps in becoming an Aztec priestess as well as how young women left the service upon marriage.

"There were also women who served in the temples since they were very young, for the reason that the mother, perhaps, offered them while very small, to the service of the temple as an act of (special) devotion. As soon as they (the babies) were between twenty to forty days old, they were presented to the one who was in charge . . . and who was something like a curate [priest]. They (the mothers) brought brooms for sweeping, a clay incensory, and incense called white copalli. All this they gave to the curate. Then this latter returned the baby to the mother and recommended very earnestly that she take great care in the bringing up of her daughter and he also reminded her to go every twenty days to the Calpuko or parish of her district and make an offering of brooms, copal and firewood for the hearths of the temple. As soon as that child attained the age of understanding, being informed by her mother about her votive offering, she went of her own free will to the temple where the other maidens were and took her offering with her, which consisted of an incensory and copal. From that time on until she was of marriageable age she lived in the temple under the tutelage of the matrons who educated the maidens. When she was of the age to have a suitor and such a one asked her in marriage, the parents and chiefs of the district having approved of the marriage, they prepared the offering, which was to be made and which consisted of quails, incense, flowers, smoke sticks, and a clay incensory, as well as prepared food. They then took the girl and led her in front of the priests of (her) temple. . . . After the reasons were given on one part and the other [about why she was leaving], the parents of the girl took their daughter home with them."

Other enemy warriors were allowed to go to their deaths fighting, even though there was no chance of winning. Anthropologist Ross Hassig, author of *Aztec Warfare*, describes this sacrificial method:

> Some captives, usually nobles and great warriors, were sacrificed in gladiatorial combat. The captive was taken to the round sacrificial stone, where he was painted with stripes. [He was also tied to the stone by one foot.] He was given four cudgels to throw, a shield, and a sword with its obsidian blades replaced by feathers. After drinking octli, he fought warriors—several, if he was a great warrior. First he fought four warriors of the military orders in a row—two jaguars and two eagles—and if he triumphed over each, he then fought all four together. If he still triumphed, then he fought a left-handed warrior. He fought until he was felled, whereupon he was stretched on his back, his chest was cut open, and his heart was torn out and dedicated to the sun. Then the body was flayed, and the skin was worn by the priests.[66]

Other Sacrificial Rites

Aztec religious rites also included ceremonies in which men, women, and children were singled out for sacrifice. One of these was an annual festival honoring the powerful Aztec god, Tezcatlipoca. A year prior to each festival, a group of handsome captive warriors was assembled in Tenochtitlán. From that group, Aztec priests selected the most perfect-looking warrior to represent Tezcatlipoca at the next festival. The chosen warrior lived in luxury for the year before being sacrificed in an elaborate ceremony. (Warriors who were not chosen were later sacrificed without such benefits.)

During the year before the festival, the chosen warrior was treated with reverence by everyone, including the emperor. He was taught to play the flute, to walk with grace, and to be charming and gracious as escorts conducted him about the city. Shortly before his death, he was married to four captive slave women who took him to an island and prepared him for his final hours. When the time came to die, he walked up the steps of the temple in front of great crowds, breaking his pottery flutes as he went. At the top he was seized by the priests' assistants and slain in the same manner as war captives.

At festivals honoring Aztec goddesses, young women captives were sacrificed. Spanish priest Bernardino de Sahagún describes a festival dedicated to the salt goddess, the patron of salt workers. A young slave woman was dressed in the likeness of the goddess and forced to participate in ten days of festivities preceding her sacrifice. Sahagún reports:

> The singing commenced towards evening and lasted until midnight, and the woman destined to die danced and sang with the others during these ten days, and after that a whole night without rest or sleep. She was held by the arms of two old women, who danced with her that entire night. The slaves who were to die in front of her and over whose bodies she was to walk in the morning to her death, danced and kept vigil the same length of time.[67]

Children also were sacrificed at certain festivals, especially those honoring Tlaloc, the rain god. Everyone was saddened by the sacrifice of children, but the Aztecs believed Tlaloc demanded the souls of children and the Aztecs needed rain. The more the doomed children cried, it was said, the more abundant the rainfall would be that season.

Among other reasons, some children were selected for sacrifice because they were born on unlucky days or born with a cowlick in their hair. The young victims were taken to the temple a few weeks before the time of the festival. Supposedly, the priests purchased them from their parents, but Sahagún says that parents of these marked children had little choice and suffered great sorrow. Their only consolation was that the souls of their children went to a heavenly paradise after death.

Sacrifices at Special Events

In addition to daily sacrifices to the sun and monthly sacrifices at religious festivals, certain important events called for mass sacrifices. One of these was the coronation of a new emperor. When the council of nobles chose a new emperor, he first had to prove his ability as a warrior and leader by conducting a military campaign. When Tizoc, an ineffective emperor, was assassinated in 1486, his brother, Ahuizotl, was chosen to replace him. In his precoronation military campaign, Ahuizotl conducted a devastating march through several territories to discourage rebellion and reinstate the power of the empire after Tizoc's weak leadership. At the same time he took many captives to sacrifice at his coronation ceremony. Historian Richard F. Townsend writes:

His campaigns were marked by swift, murderous action and ruthless retribution against his enemies. His first action—the coronation war—was to lead the allied army on a circuit into the Toluca Valley and northward to Xilotepec before turning back into the northern Valley of Mexico. This foray had the desired effect of putting down rebellious communities while reasserting strong leadership for the demoralized army. The successful fulfillment of these two aims was underlined by the booty and prisoners obtained. The triumphant conclusion of Ahuizotl's coronation saw unprecedented gift giving and feasting on a scale said to equal the tribute of an entire year. As was customary, the prisoners were sacrificed in the final act of the coronation rite.[68]

Later in his reign, Ahuizotl put on an even greater extravaganza for the dedication of the newly rebuilt temple in the center of Tenochtitlán. At that event, a steady line of captives moved silently up the steps of the temple to their deaths on the sacrificial stone. For four days the line continued its march. Thousand were killed and their severed skulls placed on the racks near the temple. In 1503, at Ahuizotl's funeral, two hundred slaves from his own household were killed to serve him in the afterlife.

Reason for Sacrifice

In his history of the Aztecs, written in the sixteenth century, Father Sahagún stated that he would not "try to disprove or discuss" the sacrificial festivals of the Aztecs, but to "simply relate the facts in their proper order."[69] In Book II of the *Florentine Codex*, he does just that, never questioning or speculating on the reasons for the rituals.

Today, however, scholars from many disciplines often reflect on the sacrificial practices of the Aztecs. They point out that innumerable societies all over the world have practiced

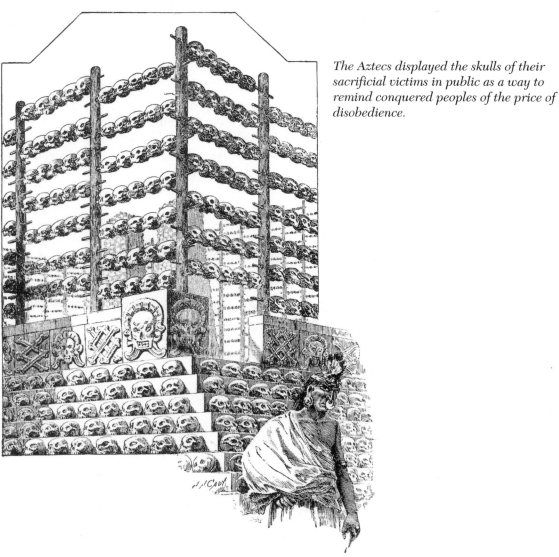

The Aztecs displayed the skulls of their sacrificial victims in public as a way to remind conquered peoples of the price of disobedience.

human sacrifice at one time or another, but rarely to the degree reached by the Aztecs. As Davies observes, the sacrifice of captives gradually came to be a matter of "one-upmanship" among succeeding emperors. "Where the Aztecs perhaps differed," Davies writes, "was in subjecting sacrifice to a kind of inflationary process whereby, if previously one or perhaps ten victims were needed to achieve a certain end or to propitiate a particular god, a thousand now had to be immolated."[70]

While no one denies that religion played a basic role in Aztec sacrifices, some scholars feel that additional factors also played a part. One of these was the Aztecs' desire to underscore the fact that their empire was rich and powerful and that resistance to its demands had unpleasant consequences. For instance, leaders of newly conquered provinces were forced to come to Tenochtitlán to watch their own warriors being sacrificed at postwar ceremonies.

The Aztecs themselves either participated in festivals that ended in sacrifice or were obliged to attend them. From childhood on, Aztecs witnessed scores of people being sacrificed in terrifying rites. While they became hardened to it in some degree, the cumulative effect was a kind of doomsday attitude that life was dangerous, uncertain, and short. Nowhere was this feeling better exemplified than in the New Fire Ceremony, held once every fifty-two years.

New Fire Ceremony

When the gods met at Teotihuacán and created the fifth world, it was said to be the very last world. The only way to keep the fifth and final world from destruction was by obedience, devotion, and sacrificial offerings to the gods. If people failed in these obligations, the world would end violently by earthquakes and human beings would be devoured by monsters from the sky. To relieve the fear that such a catastrophe could happen at any time, a New Fire Ceremony was held on the last day of a fifty-two-year cycle. On that day, the gods indicated whether the world would continue for another fifty-two years. If it did continue, then every-

Rededication of the Great Temple

When the great temple pyramid in Tenochtitlán was rebuilt and rededicated in 1487, the newly crowned emperor, Ahuizotl, exceeded all previous records for numbers of captives slain in Aztec religious ceremonies. To obtain captives for sacrifice, he conducted a series of military campaigns. In an excerpt from *The Aztecs*, author Richard F. Townsend describes the four-day carnage.

"Once again the Aztec army returned victorious [from a military campaign], this time with the intention of staging another grand ceremony to rededicate the Great Pyramid of Tenochtitlan. . . . Renovation of this building had taken place during the reign of Motecuhzoma I, and now, in 1487, another expansion was complete. The rededication of the looming structure was orchestrated by Ahuizotl as a reaffirmation of the imperial mission by staging a sacrifice that would forever remain the most terrifying occasion in the ritual life of Tenochtitlan. Prisoners of war were lined along the length of the causeways into the city, and in numbers entirely unprecedented the sacrifices continued remorselessly for four days. Appalled ambassadors from foreign nations were summoned to witness the dreadful slaughter, and the population of Tenochtitlan stood in awe in the plazas facing the pyramid. Streams of blood poured down the stairway and sides of the monument, forming huge pools on the white stucco pavement. The accounts of the Aztec elders still conveyed a sense of horror 50 years later, when their descriptions were recorded by Spanish friars and historians. Ahuizotl turned sacrifice into a powerful political lesson, instilling terror in the hearts of enemies and insuring the sensibilities of his own population to new thresholds of violence. The renewal of the building and the idea of ritually nourishing the sun and the earth now more than ever were also used to affirm the renewal of Tenochtitlan's warlike intentions."

one could breathe easier until the end of the next cycle. Psychologically, the New Fire Ceremony took the edge off the doomsday frame of mind that was ever-present in Aztec culture.

The fifty-two-year cycle was derived from the two Aztec calendars. When the day count calendar of 260 days was meshed with the solar calendar of 365 days, it took 18,980 days (fifty-two years) before the two calendars came back to their original positions. During the last few days of a fifty-two-year cycle, the tension was unbearable. People passed the time by cleaning their houses and extinguishing hearth fires, discarding the statues of their gods and their old household goods, and generally getting ready to start anew if the world continued.

On the last night of the fifty-two-year cycle, a procession of high priests and nobles led by the emperor made its solemn way from Tenochtitlán to a mount called the Hill of the Star, a distance of seven miles. Great crowds of people in Tenochtitlán and nearby cities gathered on rooftops and in public places to await the crucial moment. From the hilltop, the emperor, high priests, royal astronomers, and nobles nervously watched the heavens to see if a certain group of stars (now called the Pleiades) would cross the zenith in the customary manner. When the stars moved past that mark, astronomers signaled that the world was safe for another fifty-two years. Precisely at that moment, a captive warrior was thrown on a sacrificial stone and a fire was kindled on his chest with a fire drill (a stick used to kindle hearth fires). Archaeologist Michael E. Smith describes what happened next:

Once a flame was lit, the victim was sacrificed and his heart was thrown into the fire. The fire was carried to a temple in Tenochtitlan, where it was used to light many carefully made torches. Warriors, messengers, and other swift runners took up the torches to carry the flame to all parts of the empire. Eventually, everyone's hearth was relit from the new fire. People everywhere rejoiced at the start of a new 52-year cycle, and they obtained new household goods to begin again.[71]

Another Perspective

The excesses of Aztec warfare and religious practices often overshadow the many accomplishments of the Aztec people, making it difficult to visualize them going about their daily tasks, teaching their children, enjoying good times, and supporting each other in illness and sorrow. This sentiment is expressed eloquently by archaeologist Eduardo Matos Moctezuma:

It is erroneous to think of Aztec society and religion as concerned only with violence and aggression. . . . Nahuatl speaking peoples worked cooperatively in farming communities, developed exquisite crafts and art forms, sponsored poetry festivals, cared deeply for children, worried about the power of gossip, loved telling stories, and warmed to the excitement, color, and tensions of the marketplace. As one of the priests wrote after spending twenty years with the Mexicas, "no people love their children as much as these people." All of these activities, the human life cycle, cultural displays, farming, and trading, were regulated and renewed by ceremonial performances.[72]

In 1519, the greatest fear of the Aztec people was about to be realized—the destruction of their world. The rest of the world would go on, even the sun would survive, but when Captain Cortés stepped ashore on the east coast of Mexico, the world as the Aztecs knew it was about to end.

For many years, scholars have pondered why a battle-hardened warrior and capable leader like Montezuma II allowed Cortés and his small army to walk peacefully into the Aztec capital city instead of killing the intruders as soon as they landed on the coast. A reason often cited for Montezuma's hesitation is that he thought Cortés might be Quetzalcoatl, a powerful god revered not only by the Aztecs, but by many other Mesoamerican peoples as well.

According to legends passed down for centuries, Quetzalcoatl (also known as the feathered serpent) was a benevolent god who created the people of the fifth Aztec world. By contrast, his brother, Tezcatlipoca, was a fearsome and evil god who brought war and sorrow to the people. A great struggle arose between the brothers in which Quetzalcoatl was humiliated and defeated. Quetzalcoatl fled to the east coast of Mexico where he sailed away on a raft of entwined snakes. Another version of the legend says he sacrificed himself in a fire and was taken up into the heavens. In both versions, Quetzalcoatl vowed to return and reclaim his kingdom.

The story of Quetzalcoatl undoubtedly was known to Emperor Montezuma, who was constantly seeking signs and omens foretelling the future. Therefore, when conquistador Hernán Cortés and his army suddenly appeared on the same coast from which Quetzalcoatl departed, Montezuma was understandably alarmed. If Cortés really was Quetzalcoatl, Montezuma could ill afford to offend him. He therefore sent messengers with luxurious gifts to Cortés, and allowed him to continue his relentless march toward the capital city.

As Cortés and his men began to move inland, they fought many skirmishes and pitched battles against hostile Indians. When Cortés realized how greatly the people in the conquered regions feared and hated the Aztec, however, he convinced many of them to stop fighting him and join the march to Tenochtitlán. When Cortés, his army, and his Indian supporters arrived at the gates of the city, Montezuma came out to meet them. Still uncertain about Cortés's identity, Montezuma allowed Cortés and his men to enter the city where they were quartered in luxurious apartments.

Many of Montezuma's nobles were suspicious of Cortés's motives and urged the emperor to take action against him before it was too late. Suspecting that the nobles were plotting against him, Cortés and several of his lieutenants boldly took Montezuma hostage in his own palace. After a tense impasse lasting several weeks, the Aztecs had had enough. Fighting broke out and in the confusion, Montezuma was accidentally killed, or perhaps murdered. Enraged, the Aztecs attacked full force, and Cortés and his men were driven out of the city with great loss of life.

Once the Spaniards were expelled from Tenochtitlán, however, the Aztecs did not pursue them or follow up their military advantage while they had the chance. Cortés and the remainder of his battered army regrouped and enlisted the aid of more Indian peoples who were anxious to be rid of the Aztecs. After months of preparation, the Spaniards and their Indian allies laid siege to Tenochtitlán and literally starved out the defenders. When the Spanish army finally broke through the city's defenses in 1521, they razed and burned the capital city. Only three years after being driven from Tenochtitlán, Cortés had crushed the mighty Aztec Empire.

Alternative Explanations

Scholars today recognize that many factors led to the swift downfall of the Aztec Empire, most of them having nothing to do with the Quetzalcoatl legend. In fact, anthropologist Susan D. Gillespie makes the case that the legend was revised after the conquest to explain the defeat. Commenting

Aztec warriors and Spanish soldiers battle fiercely for control of Tenochtitlán in 1521. Just three years after the Spanish took the city, the vast Aztec Empire crumbled.

on Gillespie's work, historian Richard F. Townsend writes:

> Anthropologist Susan Gillespie has argued convincingly that the whole story of Cortés as Quetzalcoatl was created after the conquest by Aztec historians in an attempt to make sense of the Spaniard's arrival and victory, interpreting it as the outcome of a pattern of events established long ago. . . . Given that the Aztecs viewed history as a cycle of repeated events, it is highly plausible that their historians should have sought to explain the Aztec defeat as an inevitable event, pre-ordained by the cosmic pattern of history.[73]

While the legend of Quetzalcoatl may have influenced Montezuma's behavior toward Cortés to some degree, other more concrete factors account for the quick Spanish victory. For instance, the weapons used by the Aztecs were no match for the crossbows and swords of the Spaniards. Moreover, the Spaniards had horses which enabled them to move faster and maneuver more adeptly in battle than their foes. At first the Aztecs did not know what to make of horses, having never seen such animals before. Messengers who carried reports to the emperor described them as large deer without horns. They also marveled at (and were terrified by) huge mastiff dogs that the Spaniards also used in warfare.

Another factor that looms large in the defeat of the Aztec Empire was the willingness of Indian groups who hated the Aztecs to support Cortés. After the Spaniards fought their way out of Tenochtitlán, their numbers were drastically diminished. Without help from the enemies of the Aztecs, a Spanish victory would have been unlikely. "The collapse of the Aztec empire," Townsend comments, "was as much an Indian revolt as it was a Spanish conquest."[74]

Another reason for the downfall of the Aztecs was the rapid spread of European diseases from which the Aztecs had no natural immunity. Devastating smallpox epidemics killed thousands of people, and many others starved to death because they were too ill to find food or prepare it. Finally, cultural differences regarding warfare is a major factor that worked against the Aztecs. The Aztec goal in war was to defeat the enemy, collect tribute, and let the vanquished govern themselves as long as they followed the terms of surrender. Consequently, they were unprepared for a war of total destruction such as that waged by Cortés and his army.

The Spaniards wrote admiringly of the skill, bravery, and endurance of the Aztec people as they defended their island city to the death. As for the Aztecs themselves, an Aztec poet eloquently describes the shock, disbelief, and sorrow among the people during the last days of the empire:

> Broken spears lie in the roads;
> We have torn our hair in our grief.
> The houses are roofless now,
>   and their walls are red with blood.
> Worms are swarming in the streets
>   and plazas,
> And the walks are spattered with gore.
> The water has turned red,
>   as if it were dyed
> And when we drink it,
> It has the taste of brine.
> We have pounded our hands in despair
> Against the adobe walls,
> For our inheritance, our city,
>   is lost and dead.
> The shields of our warriors
>   were its defense.
> But they could not save it.[75]

Notes

Introduction: Beginnings

1. Richard F. Townsend, *The Aztecs*. Rev. ed. London: Thames & Hudson, 2000, p. 216.
2. Michael E. Smith, *The Aztecs*. 2nd ed. Malden, MA: Blackwell, 2003, p. 5.
3. Elizabeth Hill Boone, *The Aztec World*. Montreal: St. Remy Press, 1994, p.24.

Chapter 1: The Aztec People: Family and Society

4. Warwick Bray, *Everyday Life of the Aztecs*. London: B.T. Batsford, 1968, p. 28.
5. David Carrasco, *Daily Life of the Aztecs: People of the Sun and Earth*. Westport, CT: Greenwood Press, 1998, p. 121.
6. Smith, *The Aztecs*, pp. 137–38.
7. Boone. *The Aztec World*, p. 67.
8. Quoted in Bray, *Everyday Life of the Aztecs*, p. 36.
9. Bernal Dias, *The Conquest of New Spain*. Trans. J.M. Cohen. London: Penguin Books, 1963, p. 225.
10. Inga Clendinnen, *Aztecs*. Cambridge: Cambridge University Press, 1991, p. 165.
11. Townsend, *The Aztecs*, p. 209.
12. Bray, *Everyday Life of the Aztecs*, p. 43.

Chapter 2: Government and Law

13. Smith, *The Aztecs*, p. 185.
14. Townsend, *The Aztecs*, p. 77.
15. Dias, *The Conquest of New Spain*, pp. 224–25.
16. Dias, *The Conquest of New Spain*, p. 230.
17. Ross Hassig, *Aztec Warfare: Imperial Expansion and Political Control*. Norman: University of Oklahoma Press, 1988, pp. 207–208.
18. Smith, *The Aztecs*, p. 183.
19. Smith, *The Aztecs*, p. 254.
20. Bray, *Everyday Life of the Aztecs*, pp. 86–87.
21. Townsend, *The Aztecs*, p. 92.
22. Dias, *The Conquest of New Spain*, p. 248.
23. Quoted in Tarlton Law Library, University of Texas, "Aztec Law Before the Conquest," *Florentine Codex*, Book VI, Chapter 14, 1992. www.law.utexas.edu.
24. Diego Duran, *The History of the Indies of New Spain*. Eds. and trans. Fernando Horcasitas and Doris Heyden. Norman: University of Oklahoma Press, 1994, p. 454.
25. Duran, *The History of the Indies of New Spain*, p. 463.

Chapter 3: Education and Communication

26. Hassig, *Aztec Warfare*, p. 33.
27. Townsend, *The Aztecs*, p. 168.
28. Quoted in Bray, *Everyday Life of the Aztecs*, p. 52.
29. Bray, *Everyday Life of the Aztecs*, p. 64.
30. Townsend, *The Aztecs*, p. 203.
31. Mario Araujo, "Nahuatl Culture: Aztec Books, Documents and Writing," The Azteca Web Page, 1996. www.azteca.net.
32. Dias, *The Conquest of New Spain*, pp. 227–28.
33. Peter Nabakov, *Indian Running: Native American History and Tradition*, 1981, in "Against the Winds: American Indian

Running Traditions," Peabody Museum of Archaeology and Ethnology, Harvard University. www.peabody.harvard.edu.
34. Dias, *The Conquest of New Spain*, p. 112.

**Chapter 4:
Architecture, Arts, and Crafts**

35. Dias, *The Conquest of New Spain*, p. 218.
36. Boone, *The Aztec World*, p. 82.
37. Quoted in Bray, *Everyday Life of the Aztecs*, p. 130.
38. Bray, *Everyday Life of the Aztecs*, p. 135.
39. Hernán Cortés, *Letters from Mexico*. Ed. and trans. A.R. Pagden. New York: Grossman, 1971, p. 101.
40. Townsend, *The Aztecs*, p. 188.
41. Smith, *The Aztecs*, p. 22.
42. Smith, *The Aztecs*, p. 22.

Chapter 5: Economy

43. Bray, *Everyday Life of the Aztecs*, p. 113.
44. Dias, *The Conquest of New Spain*, p. 232.
45. Carrasco, *Daily Life of the Aztecs*, p. 156.
46. Carrasco, *Daily Life of the Aztecs*, p. 157.
47. Bernardino de Sahagún, *A History of Ancient Mexico*. Trans. and ed. Fanny Bandelier. Nashville, TN: Fisk University Press, 1932, p. 66.
48. Boone, *The Aztec World*, p. 101.
49. Townsend, *The Aztecs*, p. 179.
50. University of Virginia Health System. "Badianus: For Injury of Feet, 'Black Blood' and Heart Pain." www.med.virginia.edu.
51. Dias, *The Conquest of New Spain*, p. 232.
52. Ross Hassig, *Trade, Tribute, and Transportation: The Sixteenth-Century Political Economy of Mexico*. Norman: University of Oklahoma Press, 1985, p. 56.

Chapter 6: Warfare

53. Hassig, *Aztec Warfare*, p. 28.
54. Hassig, *Aztec Warfare*, p. 80.
55. Cortés, *Letters from Mexico*, p. 133.
56. Bray, *Everyday Life of the Aztecs*, p. 188.
57. David Carrasco and Eduardo Matos Moctezuma, *Moctezuma's Mexico: Visions of the Aztec World*. Niwot: University Press of Colorado, 1992, p. 66.
58. Hassig, *Aztec Warfare*, pp. 64–65.
59. Nigel Davies, *The Aztec Empire: The Toltec Resurgence*. Norman: University of Oklahoma Press, 1987, p. 187.
60. Duran, *The History of the Indies of New Spain*, pp. 352–53.
61. Davies, *The Aztec Empire*, p. 189.

Chapter 7: Religion

62. Smith, *The Aztecs*, p. 213.
63. Carrasco, *Daily Life of the Aztecs*, p. 116.
64. Bray, *Everyday Life of the Aztecs*, p. 153.
65. Davies, *The Aztec Empire*, p. 231.
66. Hassig, *Aztec Warfare*, p. 121.
67. Sahagún, *A History of Ancient Mexico*, p. 98.
68. Townsend, *The Aztecs*, p. 105.
69. Sahagún, *A History of Ancient Mexico*, p. 72.
70. Davies, *The Aztec Empire*, p. 219.
71. Smith, *The Aztecs*, p. 231.
72. Carrasco and Moctezuma, *Moctezuma's Mexico*, p. 135.

Epilogue

73. Townsend, *The Aztecs*, p. 18.
74. Townsend, *The Aztecs*, p. 219
75. Miguel Léon-Portilla, *The Broken Spears: The Aztec Account of the Conquest of Mexico*. Boston: Beacon Press, 1962.

Glossary

amanteca (ah man TAY ka): The Nahuatl word for feather workers, a prestigious group of artisans in Aztec society.

archaeology: The study of human culture from the evidence people leave behind. Monumental archaeology concentrates on the study of architecture, monuments, and spectacular artifacts. Social archaeology focuses on the everyday lives of people—their homes, tools, diet, recreation, and so forth. Techniques in both include excavation, surveys, and various dating methods.

atlatl (at LA tl): A spear thrower made from a stick that hooks into the end of a spear or dart. The atlatl remains in the thrower's hand while the spear is projected away from it with great force.

belt loom: A loom for weaving cloth from cotton and cactus fibers. One end was tied to a stationary object and the other was fastened around the waist of the weaver by a woven belt.

cacao beans: Large beans that grow in pods on the bark of trees in tropical areas. Among the Aztecs, the beans were used to make a highly prized chocolate drink restricted to the nobility. Cacao beans were dried and sometimes used as money in the marketplaces.

cacique (ca SEEK): A Mesoamerican term referring to leaders of small political units such as towns and villages.

calmecac (kal ME kak): Schools associated with the temples for children of the nobility. Boys and girls went to separate schools. Boys from the common class who showed great ability were sometimes allowed to attend.

calpulli or capolli (kal PUL li): A basic community division, similar to a clan, in cities and towns. Each division, under the direction of a noble, was the basis for assigning tribute quotas, maintaining public areas, conscripting soldiers, and providing schools.

chinampa (chi NAM pa): Manmade farming plots in the shallow areas of Lake Texcoco, sometimes referred to as a floating garden.

Cholula ware: A very fine kind of pottery made by artisans from Cholula, a region close to Tenochtitlan.

coa: A long-handled digging stick used for digging holes and planting crops.

cochineal: A highly prized red dye for fabric and other uses made from the dried bodies of a certain kind of insect.

codex: A manuscript book prepared by hand rather than printed. The plural is codices.

conch shell: A large marine shell on which a loud tone may be made by blowing through one end.

concubine: A mistress of the emperor or other high-status person. Concubines were not wives, but their position was legitimate and carried prescribed rights and privileges.

conquistador: A Spanish word meaning "conqueror," applied to Spanish explorers and soldiers in the Americas.

corbelled arch: A type of doorway construction frequently used in ancient Mesoamerica. It did not have a keystone and therefore was unable to support much weight.

cuicacalli (kui ka KAL li): Also called the "house of song," this special school was located at a temple. There children learned the songs and dances necessary to participate in religious festivals and ceremonies.

day count: A cyclical system for naming and numbering the days so that each day in a 260-day cycle had a different designation. This was important to the Aztecs because each day was associated with specific events, good and bad luck, and many other vital matters.

earplug or spool: Ornament worn in the ears of Aztec boys and men. A boy's ears were pierced when he was young and the holes were gradually enlarged by inserting larger plugs.

flower war: Formalized battle fought by Triple Alliance partners against their enemies during relatively peaceful times. The object was to train new warriors, keep old ones in fighting trim, and take captives for sacrifice.

glyph: A carved or painted symbol representing a real object, an idea, or a sound.

ideogram: A picture of an object that has meanings related to the object. For example, the picture of a sun can mean warmth, light, and daytime.

lapidary: Artisan who creates jewelry and other artistic objects from gemstones.

lipplug: Ornament inserted in a hole pierced underneath the lower lip of an Aztec man.

maguey (MA gway): A type of cactus with long, thick spikes that was used by the Aztecs for many purposes. Its fibers were used to make cloth and paper, and its juice was fermented into an alcoholic drink.

mayeques (may E kays): Aztec people without clan affiliation who worked as serfs on lands of the nobility.

metate (me TA ti): A slab of smooth stone with raised edges on which Aztec women ground corn for tortillas and other traditional dishes.

military societies: Special groups of warriors who had distinguished themselves in war by taking many captives and performing other acts of valor. The most prestigious were the jaguar society and the eagle society.

Nahuatl (NAH wa tl): Language of the Aztecs. It was not written down until Spanish missionaries transcribed it in the sixteenth century. Dialects of it are still spoken in Mexico.

obsidian: Black volcanic rock from which extremely sharp flakes were removed to make tools and weapons. Obsidian was also used to create beautiful artwork and jewelry.

patolli (pa TOL li): A popular gambling game played by the Aztecs. A mat with a diagram painted on it was laid on the ground. To win points, players tried to toss beans onto lucky sections of the diagram. Serious wagering often accompanied the game by adults. Children played their own version of *patolli*.

phonogram: A symbol representing a word, syllable, or speech sound.

pictograph: A picture of an object that represents the object itself with no other meaning associated with it.

pochteca (potch TE ka): Long-distance merchants.

post and lintel: A type of door construction in which two posts or columns of the same length are set up and capped with a horizontal piece on top.

projectile weapons: Any weapon that throws or shoots ammunition of some type at the enemy. Projectile weapons used by the Aztecs were bows and arrows, slings for rocks, and atlatls to throw darts.

pulque (PUL key): An intoxicating drink made from fermented maguey cactus juice. It was also called *octli* (OCT li).

shock weapons: Weapons used by Aztec warriors in hand-to-hand fighting. They include swords, clubs, and spears edged with razor-sharp chips of obsidian.

solar calendar: Aztec calendar consisting of eighteen months of twenty days each for a total of 360 days. Five "idle" days were added at the end of the year and another day was added periodically to coincide with the solar year.

telpochcalli (tel potch KAL li): A free neighborhood school associated with the temple for children of the common classes. Boys and girls attended separate schools.

titlantil (ti TLAN til): Messengers who traveled on foot throughout the Aztec Empire. Titlantil were organized into relay teams that were able to cover more than a hundred miles a day.

tlachtli (TLACHT li): A popular ball game played among the Aztecs. Besides its function as a sport, *tlachtli* was played to fortell the will of the gods.

tlatloani (tlat low AHN ee): A Nahuatl word meaning "first speaker," usually referring to the emperor.

tribute: Goods and services demanded by the Aztecs from their own provinces as well as from those they conquered.

Triple Alliance: A power bloc formed in the fifteenth century by the Mexicas and two adjoining groups—the Acolhuas and the Tenochas. The three often acted together against common enemies, but the Mexicas were predominant in the alliance.

For Further Reading

Books

Elizabeth Baquedano, *Eyewitness: Aztec, Inca, and Maya.* New York: DK, 2000. The color photographs, illustrations, and descriptions of Aztec life and culture in this book are outstanding. For upper elementary and young adult readers.

Frances F. Berdan and Patricia Rieff Anawalt, eds., *The Essential Codex Mendoza.* Berkeley: University of California Press, 1997. An abridged version of the *Codex Mendoza* published in paperback format.

Zelia Nuttall, ed., *The Nuttall Codex: A Picture Script From Ancient Mexico.* New York: Dover, 1975. *The Nuttall Codex* is named for Zelia Nuttall, who identified and published it. The codex is not of Aztec origin but was created by another group of Mesoamerican people called the Mixtecs. It is very similar to codices produced by the Aztecs, however, and copies of it are readily available in most libraries.

John M.D. Pohl, *Aztec Warrior: AD 1325–1521.* Buffalo, MN: Osprey Press, 2001. An interesting book about all phases of Aztec warfare—training, weapons, combat, tactics—written by an archaeologist who specializes in American Indian cultures.

Videos

The Conquistadors, hosted by Michael Wood. PBS Home Video, 2001. Cortés's conquest of the Aztecs is one of four historical events depicted in this video production. The other events are Pizzaro's conquest of the Incas, Orellana's discovery of the Amazon, and Cabeza de Vaca's crossing of the North American continent.

Fall of the Aztec and Maya Empire. Great Cities of the Ancient World Series, Questar, 1999. Computer graphics are used in this video to show how the cities of the Aztecs and Mayans probably looked when Europeans first saw them.

Rise and Fall of the Aztecs. 500 Nation Series, Vol. 2, Warner Studios, 1995. Volume two of this eight-part series includes a short history of the Aztec Empire. As a special feature, native speakers of Nahuatl, the language of the Aztecs, demonstrate how this ancient language sounds. (Teachers need to preview this video because it contains scenes of violence.)

Websites

Acoyauh's Aztec Lore (www.acoyauh.com). A wealth of information about the Aztecs may be accessed on this website, including sections on Aztec gods, mythology, legends, and language.

Ancient Scripts.Com (www.ancientscripts. com). Aztec picture writing is illustrated and explained on this website, which also contains important links to related sources.

The Aztec Calendar (www.ai.mit.edu). A full-color drawing of the Aztec calendar, or sunstone, is the focus of this website. The pictures are accompanied by descriptions of all the symbols carved on the stone and what they signify.

The Aztecs (www.rose-hulman.edu). An excellent website for viewing color photographs of Aztec art and architecture.

Drawings of everyday life based on historic information are also presented.

Codex Mendoza (www.geocities.com). A short but interesting explanation of the *Codex Mendoza* is presented on this website along with directions on how to read some of the Aztec symbols in it.

The Importance of Music in the Life of the Aztec People (www.dpsk12.org). Although this website consists of a study unit for elementary students, it provides little-known information about Aztec music and song for all ages.

Law in Mexico Before the Conquest (www.law.utexas.edu). Personnel from the Tarlton Law School at the University of Texas prepared a museum exhibit about Aztec law for the Columbus Quincentennial in 1992. The Internet version of the exhibit was prepared for the web by Eric Glass in 2002. Information on the website is excerpted from *Florentine Codex*, Book VI, Chapter 14, by Bernardino de Sahagún.

Museo del Templo Mayor (http://archaeology.la.asu.edu). The story of the Templo Mayor archaeological project in Mexico City is presented in this website, including photographs of the excavation and discoveries made during the project.

Painting Guide for an Aztec Army (www.balagan.org.uk). This website contains color pictures and detailed descriptions of the battle dress of Aztec warriors, from generals to foot soldiers.

Works Consulted

Books

Arthur O.J. Anderson and Charles E. Bibble, eds. and trans., *The Florentine Codex: General History of the Things of New Spain*, vols. 1–13 by Bernardino de Sahagún. Salt Lake City: University of Utah Press, 1982. A monumental work, making Father Sahagún's important history of the Aztecs available in English.

Ferdinand Anton, *Women in Pre-Columbian America*. New York: Abner Schram, 1973. Much of the information on ancient Mesoamerica concentrates on the role of rulers and warriors. Anton's book assembles data from many sources about the lives and roles of Aztec, Mayan, and Inca women.

Elizabeth Hill Boone, *The Aztec World*. Montreal: St. Remy Press, 1994. A well-written and attractive book with full-color photographs and other illustrations. The author, an art historian, emphasizes the artistic achievements of the Aztecs. The text is especially suited as an introduction to Aztec culture.

Warwick Bray, *Everyday Life of the Aztecs*. London: B.T. Batsford, 1968. Bray's book is somewhat outdated archaeologically, but the text is informative and easy to understand.

David Carrasco, *Daily Life of the Aztecs: People of the Sun and Earth*. Westport, CT: Greenwood Press, 1998. A detailed account of the daily life of the Aztecs for the lay reader, written by the director of the Mesoamerican Archive and Research Project at the University of Colorado.

David Carrasco and Eduardo Matos Moctezuma, *Moctezuma's Mexico: Visions of the Aztec World*. Niwot: University Press of Colorado, 1992. Two prominent scholars of Aztec history and culture collaborate to present a book about Aztec thought and wisdom. Beautiful photographs of Mesoamerican art treasures and paintings by Mexican muralist Diego Rivera make this an outstanding volume.

Inga Clendinnen, *Aztecs*. Cambridge: Cambridge University Press, 1991. A book for serious Aztec scholars involving not only descriptions of Aztec culture, but ideas and theories of how Aztec customs and practices evolved.

Codex Mendoza: The Mexican Manuscript Known as the Collection of Mendoza and Preserved in the Bodelian Library, Oxford. London: Waterloo & Sons, 1938. An important Aztec codex re-created after the Spanish conquest. It consists of three books: history, tribute, and the life cycle of an Aztec citizen from birth to death. Created for the king of Spain, the original was stolen by French pirates and later came into the possession of Oxford University in England, where it remains today.

Hernán Cortés, *Letters from Mexico*. Ed. and trans. A.R. Pagden. New York: Grossman, 1971. In his letters to the king of Spain, Hernán Cortés, conqueror of the Aztecs, provides firsthand accounts of Aztec life and culture from the viewpoint of a European.

——, *Five Letters 1519–1526*. Trans. J. Bayard Morris. New York: Robert McBride, 1929. Another translation of Cortés's letters to the king of Spain.

Nigel Davies, *The Aztec Empire: The Toltec Resurgence.* Norman: University of Oklahoma Press, 1987.

Bernal Diaz, *The Conquest of New Spain.* Trans. J.M. Cohen. London: Penguin Books, 1963. This memoir of a Spanish soldier in the army of conquistador Hernán Cortés is one of the few eyewitness accounts of the overthrow of the Aztecs. Diaz's book also provides valuable information about Aztec life and culture before the destruction began.

Diego Duran, *The History of the Indies of New Spain.* Eds. and trans. Fernando Horcasitas and Doris Heyden. Norman: University of Oklahoma Press, 1994. The author was a Spanish priest in Mexico in the sixteenth century who was determined to preserve the history of the Aztecs before it was lost. He gathered detailed information from interviews with Aztec nobles and commoners. Today Duran's history is an essential resource for serious scholars of Aztec history.

Emily Walcott Emmart, ed. and trans., *The Badianus Manuscript (Codex Barberini, Latin 241) Vatican Library: An Aztec Herbal of 1522.* Baltimore: Johns Hopkins Press, 1940. This large volume contains a copy of *An Aztec Herbal of 1522* found by accident in the Vatican library in Rome in 1929. The original book, small and velvet bound, contained colored illustrations and Latin descriptions of plants the Aztecs used for maintaining health and curing disease. Emmart's book provides English translations and commentary.

Brian M. Fagan, *The Aztecs.* New York: W.H. Freeman, 1984. A straightforward account of Aztec culture by a prominent archaeologist.

Ross Hassig, *Aztec Warfare: Imperial Expansion and Political Control.* Norman: University of Oklahoma Press, 1988. An excellent source about Aztec warfare, including how the army was organized, how it was mobilized in times of need, and how it marched, camped, and fought. In addition to descriptions of these activities, Hassig also offers insights and theories about the reasons for and goals of Aztec warfare.

———, *Trade, Tribute, and Transportation: The Sixteenth-Century Political Economy of Mexico.* Norman: University of Oklahoma Press, 1985. The Aztec Empire was created by warfare, but trade and tribute from conquered peoples held it together. Hassig examines how the Aztecs created a far-flung trading system in a land where there were no beasts of burdens or wheeled vehicles.

Miguel Léon-Portilla, *The Aztec Image of Self and Society: An Introduction to Nahuatl Culture.* Salt Lake City: University of Utah Press, 1992. The author is an authority on the oral literature of the Aztecs through which their ideals and wisdom were passed down. After Spanish priests transcribed the Aztec language (Nahuatl) into a written language, many of the Aztec songs and poems were written down for the first time. In this book, Léon-Portilla makes use of this literature to examine how the Aztecs saw themselves and their society.

———, *The Broken Spears: The Aztec Account of the Conquest of Mexico.* Boston: Beacon Press, 1962. Most Aztec histories were written by Europeans who wrote from a totally different perspective than the Aztecs. Through traditional Aztec literature and books written by Aztec scholars after the conquest, Léon-Portilla presents the story through the eyes of the conquered.

Bernardino de Sahagún, *A History of Ancient Mexico*. Trans. and ed. Fanny Bandelier. X vols. Nashville, TN: Fisk University Press, 1932. A translation of the first four books of Father Sahagún's monumental history of the Aztecs. The editor adds commentary and bibliographic information about Sahagún.

Michael E. Smith, *The Aztecs*. 2nd ed. Malden, MA: Blackwell, 2003. This book by an American archaeologist emphasizes social archaeology, which concentrates on the lives of common people and the artifacts they left behind. In recent years, Smith has conducted several excavations of this nature in rural areas outside of Mexico City. His book also describes discoveries of similar sites by other archaeologists. This is an important source for current archaeological research about the Aztecs.

Richard F. Townsend, *The Aztecs*. Rev. ed. London: Thames & Hudson, 2000. An up-to-date book about the Aztecs by an expert in Mesoamerica cultures before the arrival of Europeans. Many photographs, maps, and drawings and an interestingly written text make this an excellent introduction to the Aztec civilization.

George C. Vaillant, *Aztecs of Mexico: Origin, Rise and Fall of the Aztec Nation*. Garden City, NY: Doubleday, Doran, 1941. The author, was an archaeologist who worked extensively in Mesoamerica. While his book on Aztec history is outdated in regard to archaeological information, the text is still valid and interestingly written.

Websites

Foundation for the Advancement of Mesoamerican Studies (www.famsi.org). This website contains the complete text of *Narrative of Some Things of New Spain and of the Great City of Temestitan* [Tenochtitlán] *México Written by a Companion of Hernan Cortes, the Anonymous Conqueror.*

Public Broadcasting System (www.pbs.org). An excellent website about Spanish conquistadores. One segment is about the fall of the Aztec Empire. The series, created for middle and high school students, also presents information about Aztec culture.

University of Minnesota Morris (www.mrs.umn.edu/academic/history/Nahuatl). This website is a source for studies in the Nahuatl language of the Aztecs. Special sections lead the user to poetry, manuscripts, calendar signs, and the *Codex Mendoza.*

University of California at Irvine (www.lib.uci.edu). Early written records of Mesoamerica are presented on this informative website. All of the various Mesoamerican codices are illustrated and described in detail along with accounts of their origin and where they now are housed.

Index

Picture Credits

About the Author

Eleanor J. Hall has moved her residence so many times, she has lost count of the actual number—but every move brings something new and exciting to write about. Lately, however, she has been staying close to home in St. Louis, Missouri, writing curriculum guides for the Internet. One of these, written for the National Park Service, is a K–12 teacher's manual about the Lewis and Clark expedition. Recently, she cowrote a curriculum guide for all ages on airborne toxics for the Environmental Protection Agency. Hall has written six books for Lucent with topics reflecting her eclectic interests. The titles are *The Lewis and Clark Expedition, Garbage, Life Among the Samurai, Ancient Chinese Dynasties, Grizzly Bears*, and *Polar Bears*.